# Creating Your
# Lean Future State

# Creating Your Lean Future State

How to
Move from
Seeing to Doing

Tom Luyster
with Don Tapping

**Productivity** *Press*

New York

Most Productivity Press books are available at quantity discounts when purchased in bulk. For more information, contact our Customer Service Department (888-319-5852).

Address all other inquiries to:
Productivity Press
444 Park Avenue South, 7th Floor
New York, NY 10016
United States of America
Telephone: 212-686-5900
Fax: 212-686-5411
E-mail: info@productivitypress.com
ProductivityPress.com

*Library of Congress Cataloging-in-Publication Data*

Luyster, Tom.
  Creating your lean future state : how to move from seeing to doing / Tom Luyster, Don Tapping.
      p. cm.
  Includes index.
  ISBN-13: 978-1-56327-248-6 (alk. paper)
  1. Business logistics–Case studies. 2. Manufacturing processes–Case studies. 3. Production planning–Case studies. 4. Industrial efficiency–Case studies. I. Tapping, Don. II. Title.

HD38.5.L89 2006
658.5'15–dc22

                                                                          2006025436


10   09   07   06   5   4   3   2   1

# Contents

# Introduction

## Lean Background and Basics

Lean manufacturing, the American term for the Toyota Production System (TPS) popularized by James Womack at MIT, has rapidly come to stand for all that is forward thinking in manufacturing. The word itself focuses on the heart of TPS—eliminating "fat" or waste in the production process.

Anything that is not directly involved in turning raw material into value for the customer is by definition considered waste. You are lean when you have no waste, in other words when you have no resources allocated to anything other than producing value for your customer. Toyota addressed its production operations with this definition in mind and created a groundbreaking methodology, which centers on the concept of pull production.

When you analyze the pull production method you will realize that it is nothing more than an elegant solution for removing waste from every aspect of the production process and delivering quality products to customers on time and at the lowest possible cost. Figure I-1 illustrates the basic elements of pull production.

Starting with the customer order, a product is pulled through the system, moving upstream back to raw material orders. It is the reverse of what is generally known as the "push" system, which pushes material through the system from raw material to final assembly as fast as the system can move it, creating piles of raw material and work-in-process inventories everywhere. Material wait time is a primary source of waste in the push system and causes many types of costs to accumulate for no other reason than you produce because you are able to. In contrast, the discipline involved in a pull system, is to make a product only when it has been ordered and not a minute sooner.

### What's Wrong With This Idea?

Despite the undisputed success of TPS and its widely accepted pull-based methodology, there are some underlying problems with this approach. What happens, for example, if a machine goes down just when an order comes in? What if a customer

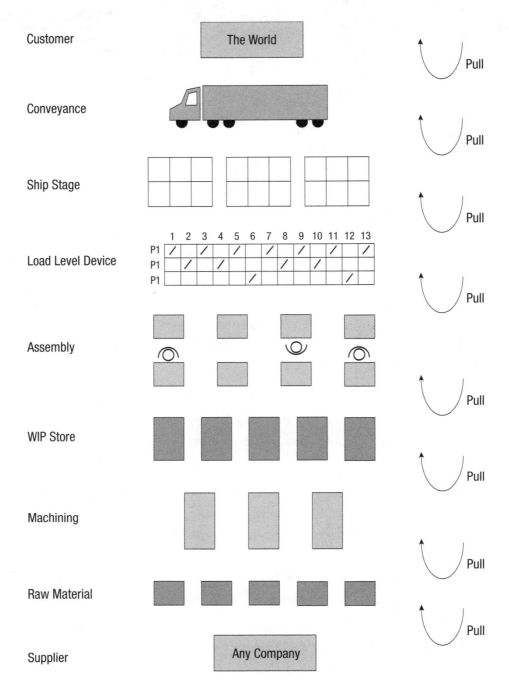

**Figure I-1.** Pull System Schematic—Customer to Supplier

orders twice the amount ordered the previous month and you don't have enough raw materials to meet the new demand? What if your supplier misses a shipment? Most companies protect themselves from these "what-ifs" by stockpiling, but this response goes against the grain of lean. The best way to avoid this is through value stream mapping, which supports a pull production system while protecting you from the what-ifs.

If you have mapped your value streams—and this workbook is written from the premise that you have—you have *learned to see the sources of waste, to see value*, and to make value flow to the customer. You have also developed a plan to implement a future state map. In fact, you and your team are chomping at the bit to hit the plant floor and implement the future state you have envisioned.

### Whoa!

Enthusiasm is a wonderful motivator, but unless you have the foundation for implementing a lean system, what you have in your hand is not an implementation plan but a plan for disaster. The value stream map and the implementation plan are a good beginning, but they are by no means the only things you will need. You must **Stabilize**, **Standardize**, and **Simplify** the processes that you are so eager to change and improve.

Most companies embarking on a lean initiative do so with the mistaken belief that their existing processes are a lot better than they really are. As they begin to implement lean, they soon discover that those processes are not in control. They also discover that shaky, unstable processes, which are supposed to support the smooth flow of products, materials, and production information, are incapable of doing so.

So the wheels fall off. The cell keeps running out of parts. It makes product based on its capacity, rather than true demand. Operators can't work to takt time, equipment fails, and deliveries are missed. Soon, operators have batches piled up between machines again, inventory is built up, a more expensive MRP system is ordered, and senior management is suspicious about lean anything. The bottom line is that there is no positive impact on the bottom line.

Mapping a value stream and creating an implementation plan for establishing the future state is no guarantee of success. Mapping is a necessary and very critical first step, but if you want implementation to stick, without backsliding, you must stabilize, standardize, and simplify. Only by doing this can you truly get the benefits promised on the future state map. It is with this underlying concept in mind that *Creating Your Lean Future State* was written; moreover, it is this underlying concept that has shaped the sequence and structure of the chapters to come.

## How to Use This Book

### Overviews

Because lean works best when it is built on the solid framework of stability, standardization, and simplification, this introduction provides an overview of each of these critical elements. Because lean planning and implementation depend on knowledge of lean as well as of some of the basic precepts that are critical to the successful implementation of lean, the introduction will also include an overview of these important precepts.

### Forms

As you proceed through this book, forms and clear instructions about how to use them accompany each step. A CD is provided with all the blank forms for your easy duplication, use, and modification. The "CD" icon is used throughout the text to indicate when you can refer to the CD-ROM for an interactive form.

### Case Studies and Future State Maps

Throughout the text, case studies based on the experiences of "SLMS Molding, Inc." are used to demonstrate the implementation process. Each form or procedure will have an example completed for the SLMS case. In each case, a corresponding future state map is highlighted to show where each step fits in the whole process.

## Overview: The Three S Model of Lean Implementation

This book distills what seems to be a complex process into a three-step system: *a Three S Model* that consists of stabilization, standardization, and simplification. Because these three Ss are the focus of the implementation method described in this book, a brief description of how each fits into the process is presented below.

### I. Stabilize—Demand and Process

Production is designed and controlled according to the demands of your customers. Chapter 1 of this book starts with a focus on demand planning and takes you through the essential steps of customer evaluation and teaches you to evaluate customer sales histories and identify periods of highs and lows so that you can develop takt time and establish appropriate buffer stocks.

Because you must also make certain that material handlers can complete their routes from material stores to assembly in time for work to take place, you must determine how often the handlers should take parts from assembly to shipping. Both are related to establishing "pitch," which is also covered in this chapter.

Moreover, you must evaluate your own operations, in terms of labor, machine capacity and capability as well, so that you understand clearly what you must do to meet customer demand and establish appropriate buffer and safety stocks. Each of these is covered in Chapter 2.

## II. Standardize—Visuals and Methods

Implementing continuous flow manufacturing throughout your plant ensures that both internal (downstream) and external customers receive the right product, at the right time, and in the right quantity. Transforming information and manufacturing processes into visual systems that support flow ensures that production will occur only in response to customer demand that "pulls" from upstream processes.

Chapter 3 explains the elements of a visual layout, including cell design, supermarkets, and a visual address system. Chapter 4 addresses the visual production process, kanban systems, and standardized work that are the heart of a lean operation.

## III. Simplify—Process and Introduction of Effective Kaizen

Stabilize and standardize may be mutually dependent and can parallel each other. Through stabilization, you generate labor, materials, equipment, and space savings. Through standardization, you put in place phase labor, process uptime, flow, and visuals, further advancing stabilization gains. Methods for processes and procedures are standardized across shifts, eliminating duplication of effort and excess equipment. The simplification process continuously improves the value stream. When you pace the flow, new discoveries are made and changes instituted. These changes can be simple, ten-minute kaizen events. Other discoveries based on your lean experience can lead to dramatic changes in a future program. It is important for everyone in the organization to understand that it may take up to two years to "see" the results of lean efforts.

As shown in Figure I-2, these three stages of lean implementation have numerous steps, which will be described in detail as you proceed through this book. The approach laid out in these three sections incorporates the entire value stream. Each step must be completed; some may be done in sequence, others may be done concurrently. In each case, you can relate the system described here to your own situation. If something does not make good business sense or seems unreasonable for your environment, don't do it! Look for another way to solve problems or address concerns.

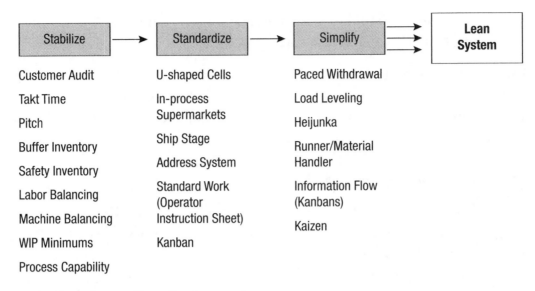

**Figure I-2:** Three Stages of Lean Implementation

A cautionary note here is to avoid the temptation to view anything difficult as unreasonable or undoable. Implementing lean will challenge most, if not all, of your assumptions about manufacturing and will force you to discover how to achieve the impossible. If you are not committed to lean, you will wind up with a pat excuse for sidestepping tough actions, and your lean conversion will wilt. The purpose of this workbook is to make it bloom.

## Overview: Teams and Tools

### The Implementation Team

Many organizations shy away from assigning staff to a dedicated lean team. Cost is usually cited as the main reason for this, but it is not a valid reason. A lean team member's cost can be treated the same as a capital expenditure; it will be amortized in weeks or months (not years) while the team generates savings, and those savings will continue to flow to the bottom line in greater proportion as the team gains experience.

The team you select to lead the implementation of your future state must be relieved of all other duties so they can focus on their task. Support personnel (quality, materials, planning, maintenance, etc.) must be advised by senior management that they are "on call" and can be tagged by the team to take action in response to a given team project. The team may include one hourly person from the target value stream and a leader with good common sense.

## Value Stream Management

Value stream management (VSM) provides a powerful tool for planning your lean implementation.[1] VSM links strategic plans to daily work. It is a process for planning and linking lean initiatives through systematic data capture and analysis and represents the most well-developed method for planning a lean transformation. If you hope to create an authentic lean enterprise, knowing the system and *knowing it extremely well* is the name of the game. This means knowing what lean tools and methods do and how to integrate them into your processes. A brief summary of VSM will help you determine what you need to have in place before launching your lean implementation. The eight steps of the VSM process are listed below and then briefly described.

1. Commit to lean
2. Choose the value stream
3. Learn about lean
4. Map the current state
5. Determine lean metrics
6. Map the future state—demand, flow, and leveling
7. Create kaizen plans
8. Implement kaizen plans

### Commit to lean

Commitment to lean requires 100 percent buy-in: total commitment from the top, total involvement on the floor. Managers can't give the order to become lean and then expect it to happen. They must be involved from the beginning and throughout with the implementation. The ideas that ensure success will come from the people who do the work; without management support, these people will be reluctant to commit to the change process.

To reduce and eliminate waste effectively, employees must be behind the lean transformation effort. They can't be afraid that improving their jobs will cost them their jobs! Ensuring their support starts with communication between top management and all levels of the organization. A core implementation team must be selected with

---

1. For more on value stream management see the book *Value Stream Management: Eight Steps to Planning, Mapping, and Sustaining Lean Improvements* by Don Tapping, Tom Luyster, and Tom Shuker (Productivity Press, 2002), and the *Value Stream Management* video set, created by Don Tapping, Tom Fabrizio, and the Productivity Press Development Team (Productivity Press, 2001).

someone from management as well as someone from the line as members; this team will be responsible for keeping the lines of communication open. From the beginning, top management must articulate the need to become lean. Once everyone understands the need, top management must find ways to open doors, allowing others in the organization to contribute to their full capacity.

It is important to participate as much as possible in the initial phases of your lean implementation. Lean is not just a different approach to running the front line; it is a different approach to work and to management-worker relationships. Full commitment is the only thing that will get you through the rough moments that accompany the transformation.

### Choose the value stream

A value stream consists of everything—including non-value-adding activities—that occur in turning raw materials into finished goods. There are many value streams within an organization, just as there are many rivers flowing into an ocean. A value stream encompasses all the actions—both value-added and non-value-added—that are necessary to bring a product from raw material through the manufacturing process to receipt of payment. In manufacturing, each product family is considered a separate value stream. The VSM process helps you systematically identify and eliminate the non-value-adding elements. The appropriate value stream selection depends on your plant and customer demand. You should select a value stream that needs to be improved due to poor profits, falling market share, cost reduction demands, or as a benchmark for the rest of your operations.

### Learn about lean

This step in VSM ensures that everyone—from senior management down to the shop floor—has a strong enough understanding of lean concepts and terms to complete the VSM planning process. During implementation, you will find that education and training are critical to success. Your core implementation team will need to understand all the tools of lean manufacturing and will help you identify who else needs to be trained and when. Moreover, as the lean implementation gets underway, workers will be asking to learn more, and you will want to be ready with a variety of programs and resources that can be used to raise their level of understanding and skill. A number of training tools can be used: simulations, benchmarking, studies of successful in-house projects, books and videos, consultants, and group discussions.

## Map the current state

A value stream map gives a visual representation of the material and information flow for a product family and is an indispensable tool for managing process improvements. To improve a process, you must first observe and understand it. By mapping a process you get a clean picture of the wastes that inhibit flow. Eliminating the waste makes it possible to reduce manufacturing lead time, which will help you meet customer demand.

The current state map puts a stake in the ground; it should reflect *accurate, real-time data* related to the targeted value stream. The collection of data for a current state map starts with the shipping department (the closest point to the customer) and works upstream through the various processes. This will help you observe and understand the value stream from your customer's perspective. Common value stream mapping icons are shown in Figure I-3.

One of the keys to establishing lean flow is to understand how production scheduling is achieved. Capturing details about information flow as well as material flow is the

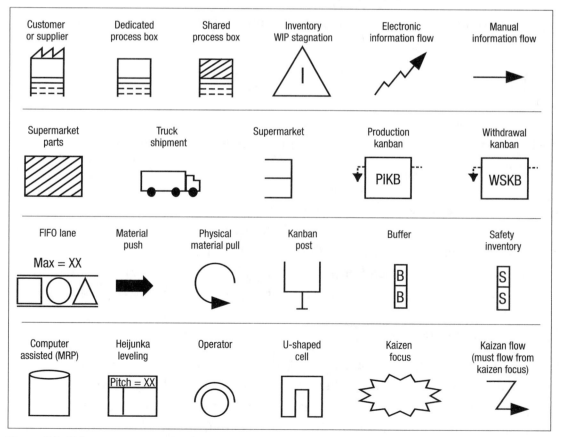

**Figure I-3.** Value stream mapping icons

essence of value stream mapping. Ask questions like, "How do you know what to make next?" and turn the answers into visual elements of the current state map.

The core implementation team maps the current state by drawing rough sketches of the production area, going to the floor to collect actual process data, and entering the information on the map using standard icons. The mapping process helps you visualize the entire manufacturing flow, not just single isolated operations. Everyone on the team must agree that the map is accurate and reflects the current reality; it is then posted for all to see.

### Determine lean metrics

The best way to get people to contribute to lean initiatives is to give them a way of seeing the impact of their efforts. Lean metrics provide the means to drive your continuous improvement efforts. The metrics that are right for your organization depend a great deal on your circumstances, but there are several common key measures that every lean-bound organization should utilize:

- Parts per labor-hour
- Inventory turns within the value stream and total plant
- Defective internal and external parts per million (PPM) (a Total Quality Management [TQM] program)
- Uptime and operational efficiency (OE) based on demand (Total Productive Maintenance [TPM])
- Labor turnover
- Pitch attainment (adherence to takt image, the vision of true one-piece flow through the entire plant)

In lean, these metrics may focus on different things than they do in a typical push production system. Make sure you understand the differences. Once you have determined which metrics to use, calculate baseline measures from the data collected in the mapping process. Remember that people react to what they are measured on, so make certain that the measurements you put in place achieve the desired results!

### Create a future state map

Creating the future state map is the heart of VSM. Focus on the three S model described in this book (stabilize, standardize, simplify) and design the future state according to demand, flow, and leveling. Understanding customer demand helps you *stabilize* your operations so that you can meet demand without producing too

## Current State Maps and Future State Maps: A Case Study

### THE CASE OF SLMS MOLDING, INC.

SLMS was a traditional batch manufacturer. Similar machines were grouped together in departments. Parts were moved from department to department in large batches for processing. One of the company's products—a top and bottom support arm—was supplied to DC Manufacturing, Inc., an automotive assembly plant. The support arm was assembled in a general assembly area at SLMS. (See the Current State Map in Figure I-4 for details of the SLMS plant before lean was implemented.)

In this state, material handlers brought raw stock to the lines in large quantities. The raw stock initially went through molding, where three injection-molding presses, each staffed by a molding department operator, made the support arms. Presses ran three shifts to supply parts to the painting operation and directly to assembly.

Changeovers took approximately two hours. Changing the plastic color took 15 to 20 minutes. Occasionally a manager considered cutting changeover times. It was more of a "nice-to-do" idea, rather than a "have-to-do." Now and again, someone wondered, "Why change colors when you don't have to?" All in all, however, managers believed that when a tool was in a press and running, all was good. Run it, run it, run it.

After about a week, the molded parts were painted. A robotic painting operation painted the "arms" in big batches. The paint line was 120 racks long with three plastic parts to the rack. The company could paint everything in one shift, so it did. After another delay, the painted parts went through assembly, then ultimately continued on to shipping.

Supervisors told operators what to make on a daily basis and considered their primary responsibility to be keeping operators busy. When the skids at the end of the line were filled with product, the material handlers transported them to the warehouse. From there, they were shipped to the customer daily. Management kept the raw material warehouse filled to make sure stockouts didn't stop production.

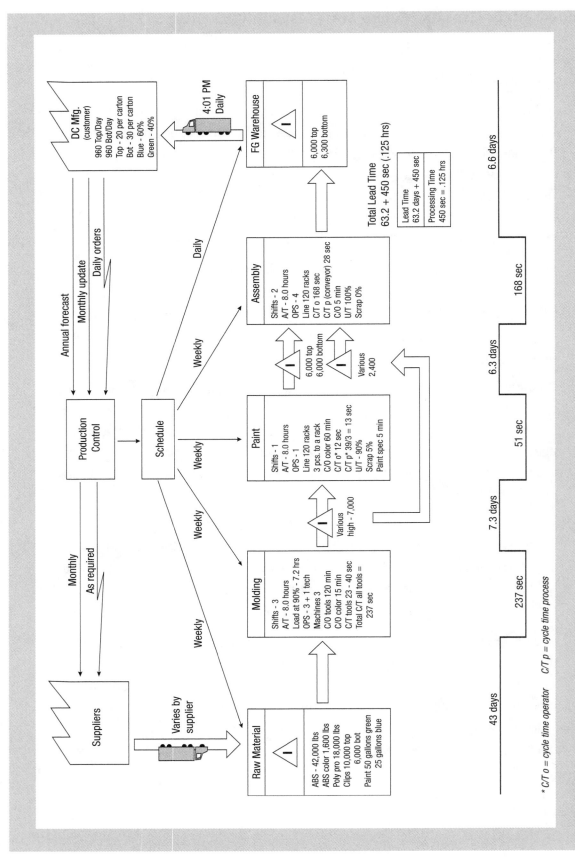

**Figure 1-4.** Current State Map

From a value stream standpoint, SLMS had a total product lead time of about 63 days, including 43 days in raw material storage, more than six days in finished goods inventory, and approximately 13 days of work in process (WIP) in molding, paint and assembly. Obviously, the operation was far from lean.

The need for change became evident after customers began complaining about prices. DC Mfg., Inc., SLMS' primary customer for support arms, announced that it wanted a price reduction. SLMS had little chance of meeting customer cost-down requirements without dramatic change, and since some SLMS managers had been to a few seminars on lean manufacturing, the company decided that this might be the way to go.

Some managers had heard about value stream mapping at industry conferences and decided that this was a good place to start. They mapped their current state and then their proposed future state (see Figure I-5). With some skepticism and occasional spells of outright terror, they began their lean implementation. They have never looked back.

much or too little. Then create a flow of information and product through your operations and *standardize* your operations to maintain that flow. Leveling is the final step that *simplifies* production control so that it paces production to the rhythm of customer demand.

A sample future state map is provided at the end of this introduction. In subsequent chapters, this map will be used to illustrate the specific concepts covered in the text.

## From Seeing to Doing

The current and future state maps give you a precise view of your production operations; however, it is not enough to see what needs to be done. Once you have your plan, you have to make it happen. This book picks up where VSM ends. It is designed to help you move from *seeing* what you need to do to *doing* what you need to do. The case study presented below illustrates how the points addressed in this introduction coalesce into a workable methodology; the chapters that follow dissect the distinct facets of the methodology and provide specific guidelines for making it work.

Figure I-5 is the future state map for SLMS Molding, Inc. The map calls for combining assembly and paint operations, with three molding machines supplying the com-

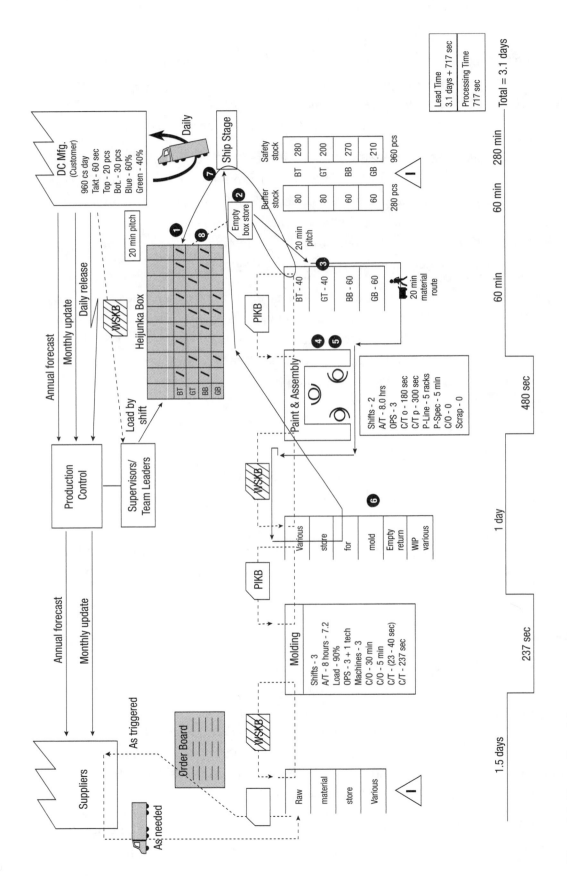

**Figure I-5.** Future State Map

bined assembly/paint operation. The map also calls for a supermarket between the press and the new assembly operation. The future state envisions a total cycle time of slightly more than three days. (Note: In this future state map, the total cycle time for the molding operation is unchanged, even though changeover times have been reduced, because of the technical parameters of a molding operation. In a different operation, changeover times might reduce cycle times.)

To implement this future state, SLMS had to have a solid foundation for its new assembly cell and pull system before moving equipment. The company also had to **understand customer demand thoroughly**—not just from the perspective of takt time! It had to know how much value-adding labor was required in assembly. It had to decide on a system for storing WIP so material handlers could find it. For that matter, it had to know how much WIP was really needed. Above all, SLMS had to have an accurate uptime estimate for the molding machines, *before* creating the assembly cell.

This is a good time to look at the future state map for a value stream in your own organization. Have all of the above issues and questions been resolved? Later in this workbook, you will see how SLMS resolved these issues and others to stabilize and standardize operations in the process of implementing its pull production plan. The book also provides all the forms needed to get you through each step, with instructions and additional illustrations from the SLMS case study. This is the grunt work of implementing lean manufacturing—the difference between success and failure.

# Stage I. Stabilize

Lean manufacturing starts and ends with the customer. Before you make any changes in your organization, on the plant floor or anywhere else, you must understand what the customer is asking you to supply. Customer demand determines what you must produce. If you are going to get your costs down, eliminate the waste in your operations and processes, and deliver quality products on time in the shortest possible time, then you will have to stabilize your operations at every point so that swings in demand can be handled without toppling the entire system.

Lean manufacturing, and pull production in particular, are very sensitive systems. They can turn on a dime with demand as long as you have built some **stability** into your system as well. This section discusses how to analyze your customer demand, build buffer and safety stocks that can stabilize your operations in relation to demand and still maintain minimum WIP on the floor, and understand your own operations. The three key components of this phase of implementing lean manufacturing—customer evaluation, self-evaluation, and process stabilization—are covered in Chapters 1 and 2. Team members can collect data about the first two simultaneously and then address the third.

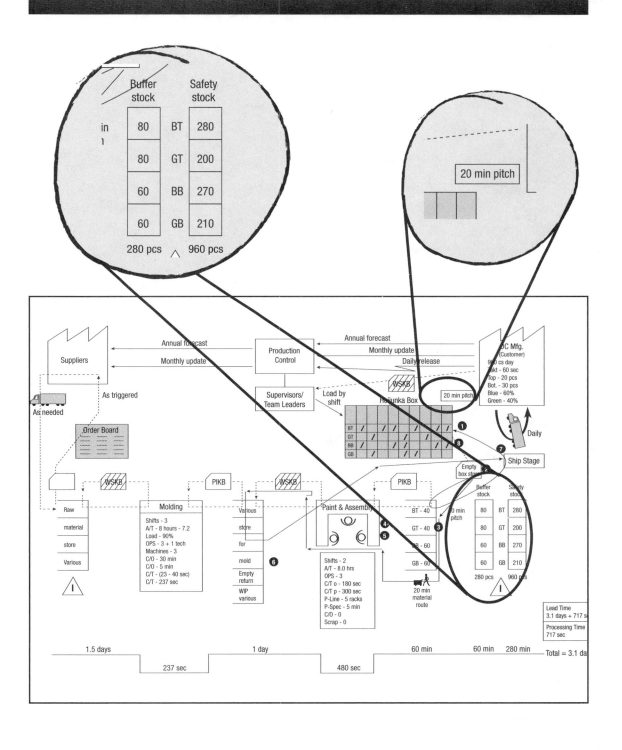

# Chapter 1. Demand Planning

Value stream maps are most useful if they are limited to and defined by the specific parameters of a specific value stream. Thus, it is important to choose only one product, or product family, to work on at a time. You may, for example, make similar parts (e.g., rear view mirrors) for Toyota, Ford, GM, and Daimler-Chrysler. But because each of these four customers has unique specifications, you have four value streams. Determining which of these value streams should be targeted for lean implementation first is often a simple matter of listening to customers: The customer demanding improvement points out which stream becomes the first target area. Once this decision has been made, you will need to focus on customer evaluation. There are four things to consider when approaching this task:

1. Customer demand
2. Takt time
3. Pitch
4. Buffer and safety stocks

## Customer Demand

### What Is Demand?

Customer demand is one of the most critical, yet misunderstood, building blocks of your lean foundation. Your accurate analysis of the demand history/future requirements and variation is very important to the initial success of the lean program. It will be the base for establishing takt time, which will then be used for future calculations of labor, material lot size, material handler loop, pitch, and capital equipment requirements. Some managers become overwhelmed by the potential variety of similar products, but you will find that the actual variety is not as overwhelming as you may fear. Experience shows, for example, that if you have 3,000 colors in your pallet portfolio, demand will invariably focus on only a few of these. One tool that makes this potential demand variety less intimidating is three-R categorization:

**Runners:** The products that have the most frequent demand

**Repeaters:** The products that have less frequent demand

**Rogues:** The products that have sporadic or very infrequent demand

Sorting potential demand variety in this way can simplify your understanding of the demand. It also simplifies establishing a baseline for your lean effort.

## What Documents and Sources Will You Use to Determine Demand?

Your sales organization should be able to supply this information and tell you how often it is updated. The more frequently it is updated, the better. In some industries a quarterly sales forecast is not frequent enough to manage the business properly when you go lean. You may need weekly forecasts. Use what is right for your business. You can use a number of internal or external production planning documents to assist you in assessing customer demand.

### The annual sales forecast

This is a forecast confirmed by at least the last two months' sales/shipment history and the next three months of customer-driven planning. The most accurate data for this forecast shows what is actually shipped to customers, not what customers said they were going to take. In addition you must determine the variation in demand for the part or product being evaluated.

### Specific product release plan or a customer order plan

If there is any type of release plan, you will probably find this information in your existing MRP/ERP system, or you can obtain it from the customer directly. Is it monthly, weekly, daily, or multiple daily?

### The customer's operating hours—one shift or more?

If your customer is also a manufacturer, you may want to match your customer's shift schedule. For instance, a customer implementing lean may run two 8-hour shifts with several hours in between. The in-between hours allow the customer to make up any production at the end of the shift rather than waiting until the end of the week. The time buffer also allows time for total productive maintenance (TPM) on equipment. When the next shift comes in, processes can begin without delay. In some cases, you may prefer not to match your customer's schedule. For example, even if your customer has a three-shift operation, you may decide to support the demand with a two-shift operation.

### Specific inventory expectations or demands

This is a tough one because your customer's expectations and demands may not be viable for you or your production environment. At times, you may have to communicate this to a customer: "You have given us the responsibility of supplying this product.

We have accepted that responsibility. But you can't demand how much inventory we must have on the floor. That is our decision. You had enough faith in us to give us the business; our responsibility is to supply you." Customers who are not yet lean may not understand what you are saying (or doing) until they reap the benefits of your low-inventory, lean system. Don't let that deter you; it is your customer who will be rewarded for your diligence.

### The customer's shipping requirements

Determine pack quantities, skid quantities, how skids should be loaded, desired pick-up frequencies and times, and any other details that may help you set up a lean shipping stage area (discussed in Chapter 3).

After gathering the information you need about your customer's order history, expectations, etc., complete a customer evaluation form (see Figure 1-1 for an example of a

**SLMS Molding, Inc.**

**Customer Evaluation Form**

Customer Evaluation: _____          Date:  2/28

Customer:  DC Mfg.                                               Program:  Strut

| Part Desc. or No. | Annual Volume | Individual products in percent of Total Volume | | | | |
| --- | --- | --- | --- | --- | --- | --- |
| | | Blue | Green | | | Volume |
| Top | 230,400 | | | | | |
| | | | | | | |
| Blue | | 60% | | | | 138,240 |
| Green | | | 40% | | | 92,140 |
| | | | | | | |
| Bottom | 230,400 | | | | | |
| | | | | | | |
| Blue | | 60% | | | | 138,240 |
| Green | | | 40% | | | 92,140 |
| | | | | | | |
| | | | | | | |
| | | | | | | |
| | | | | | | |
| | | | | | | |
| | | | | | | |

**Figure 1-1.** Customer Evaluation Form for SLMS

form including data for SLMS). This information will be particularly useful when you begin to level production (discussed in Chapter 5).

## Takt Time

From the data you collect on customer demand, you will determine your takt time: the time in which your operation must produce a single component or a finished product so that production matches the average customer demand. Producing to takt time sets the pace of production equal to the pace of sales. It also allows you to determine direct labor requirements in relation to demand. This prevents overproduction, the most serious of all manufacturing wastes.

When a plant is producing to takt time you can almost clap your hands to the production rhythm. Takt time keeps the beat of customer demand. Takt time is the time required between completions of successive units of end product; it determines how fast a process needs to run to meet customer demand.

### How to Calculate Takt Time

To calculate takt time for a particular value stream, divide the available daily production time by the total quantity required for one day (see Figure 1-2). Remember to use only available (i.e., paid) production time. If a shift is listed as 8.5 hours, but there is a 30-minute unpaid lunch, the total *available* time is 8 hours. (Note: Additional instances that may take away from available time include shopfloor meetings, breaks, lunch, and training.)

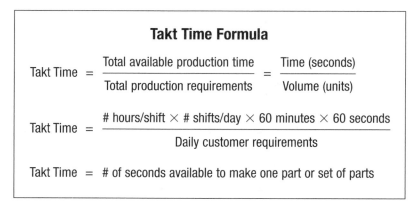

**Takt Time Formula**

$$\text{Takt Time} = \frac{\text{Total available production time}}{\text{Total production requirements}} = \frac{\text{Time (seconds)}}{\text{Volume (units)}}$$

$$\text{Takt Time} = \frac{\text{\# hours/shift} \times \text{\# shifts/day} \times 60 \text{ minutes} \times 60 \text{ seconds}}{\text{Daily customer requirements}}$$

$$\text{Takt Time} = \text{\# of seconds available to make one part or set of parts}$$

**Figure 1-2.** Takt Time Formula

Use the takt time calculation form to record the necessary information and determine your takt time. The takt time calculation form for SLMS is shown in Figure 1-3. As you can see from this figure, SLMS has a takt time of 60 seconds.

---

### SLMS Molding, Inc.
## Takt Time Calculation Form

**Takt Time** is the optimal designated time limit set for producing a single component or a finished product based on number of products sold.

To determine Takt Time, divide total available production time by total production requirements.

$$\text{Takt Time} = \frac{\text{Total available production time (seconds)}}{\text{Total production requirements (units)}}$$

> **SLMS Production Schedule**
>
> 1st Shift: 6–2:30 (8.5 hrs = 510 min)
>
> 2nd Shift: 3:30–12 (8.5 hrs = 510 min)
>
> Both Shifts:
>   20 minutes  Lunch
>   10 minutes  Break

**Calculating available production time**—(Assumes equal time for all shifts)

1. # hours in the shift: 8.5 × 60 minutes                                      = 510 minutes

2. List total time for lunch and break(s) here                                 = 30 minutes

3. Subtract lunch and break time (line 2) from shift hours (line 1)            = 480 minutes

4. Multiply line 3 by 60 seconds                                               = 28,800 seconds
   *This represents your available production time per shift*

**Calculating production requirements**

1. Determine annual probable need from customer                                = 230,400 sets

2. Determine manufacturing days per year (probably 240)

3. Divide annual need: 230,400 by mfg. days/year: 240                          = 960
   This gives you your daily production requirements

4. Divide daily production requirements by # of shifts per day
   *This gives you production requirements per shift*                          = 480

**Calculating Takt Time**

Total available production time per shift          28,800 seconds

Divide this by production requirements per shift   480

This gives you Takt Time                           60 seconds

---

**Figure 1-3.** SLMS Takt Time Calculation

## Pitch

When the actual takt time is too short or too long to establish a reasonable rate of withdrawal, you must establish an alternate method to pace the pull of material through the value stream. The name for this alternate method is "pitch," which can be simply defined as an increment of time based on takt time but adjusted for container quantities or lot sizes.

For example, your customer will probably never take away product one piece at a time; in fact, most customers want parts packed in a container. To accommodate this, you use pitch. Pitch is calculated by taking the number of pieces the customer wants in the container (called the pack-out quantity) and multiplying that number by takt time (see Figure 1-4). This gives you a lot size that is a multiple of takt time so that you can maintain a paced withdrawal.

---

**Pitch Formula**

Pitch (minutes) = Takt Time (sec) × Pack-out quantity (# pcs. in ship container) ÷ 60 sec.

*Note:* Takt Time is customer driven. Pack-out quantity may or may not be.

---

**Figure 1-4.** Pitch Formula

Applying the takt time formula to the SLMS model shows that DC Mfg. needs one set of support arms from SLMS every 60 seconds. Obviously, SLMS would not put one support arm on a truck every 60 seconds and chauffeur it to the assembly plant, and this is precisely the kind of situation that calls for pitch. Thus, if DC Mfg. wants 20 pieces in a box and the takt time is one minute, then every 20 minutes SLMS moves a box of product from final assembly to the ship stage area.

It is suggested that you try to maintain a pitch that is the shortest increment of time possible and will allow you to maintain flow. A pitch of 20 minutes is the recommended maximum unless the takt time for one unit is more than 20 minutes. Use common sense in this calculation. In the aerospace industry, for example, pitch for low-volume items may be hours instead of minutes.

### DETERMINING SLMS PITCH

SLMS's customer wanted 20 top support arms per box and 30 bottom support arms per box. SLMS could not have two pitches, or two rates of production, for the support arms or it would have shipped the customer incomplete boxes. SLMS calculated the pitch for both tops and bottoms and then used the lower of the two to set the pace. The calculation looked like this:

20 pieces x 60 sec. = 20-minute pitch

30 pieces x 60 sec. = 30-minute pitch

The pitch for the support arm is 20 minutes. Every 20 minutes the route person will take away a box containing 20 tops; a box containing 30 bottoms will be removed in sequence at the appropriate time.

SLMS chose the 20-minute pitch, as this was the shortest length of time in the pack calculations. If the company had chosen the 30-minute pitch, it would have created delays in pulling the material required in the 20-minute pitch.

## Practical Considerations for Establishing Pitch

One of the most important benefits of pacing production is that it causes problems to surface quickly. The smaller the pitch, the faster you will detect problems and the less waste you will have in your system.

Suppose a customer wanted 100 pieces packed in each container. At the same takt time of 60 seconds, there would be 100 minutes between withdrawals at the final operation. This is too long an interval between withdrawals to spot problems and respond to them. In this situation, you would break the customer's package down to a smaller lot size, perhaps 20 pieces or a fifth of the desired container. The route person would remove a container of 20 pieces every 20 minutes and put them in a master container holding the desired 100 pieces. This is a way to artificially introduce a 20-minute pitch to the line even though the customer container holds 100 pieces.

Also consider an opposite situation. Suppose the customer wants five pieces in each container. Assuming the same takt time of 60 seconds, that would reduce the pitch to five minutes, but this may not be enough time for the route person to walk the route of withdrawing finished product and replenishing it with raw material. Assuming that this person can travel this route in 10 minutes, the solution is to withdraw two boxes at a time, which produces a 10-minute pitch. The take home lesson is that route can impact pitch. The following example shows how and why to adjust pitch for maximum benefit.

Assume that the customer pack-out quantity is 10 units per box. That gives you a pitch of 10 minutes. If the route is 15 minutes, you can go to a pitch of 20 minutes. Now the route person will withdraw two containers at a time every 20 minutes. This gives you paced withdrawal timed to customer demand. More importantly, it allows the production line to be based on true takt time. The route person has an extra five minutes, but that is acceptable for now. You may, however, take this as an opportunity to kaizen the route in order to achieve a 10-minute pitch. (The material replenishment route is discussed in more detail in Chapter 5.)

### One-Piece Flow

As the example above demonstrates, pitch (and by extension, takt time) can help promote and sustain one-piece flow throughout the entire plant by identifying areas that would benefit from kaizen. For this reason, it is important to have your engineering group involved in the lean effort. This group can develop fixtures and processes that will allow you to move toward one-piece flow more rapidly. At SLMS, for instance, a lean engineering project found a way to move painting operations from a giant paint booth monument directly into assembly operations so the support arm value stream could run more closely to takt time.

You should also be aware that limitations in technology may prevent you from achieving one-piece flow. You cannot take a $500,000 injection-molding machine and have it produce at takt time; by extension, you cannot calculate pitch that will accomplish this either. It would be counterproductive to slow down such an expensive piece of capital equipment to produce once every minute.

The same holds true for a stamping press supplying multiple value streams. In these situations, the equipment will produce in batches for a "supermarket." Withdrawal from the supermarket will send a signal, such as a kanban, (discussed in Chapter 3), back to the press to make more. In this way, overproduction is kept to minimum levels.

## Buffer and Safety Stocks

Understanding your customer allows you to control inventory and stabilizes demand to the floor. *Buffer stock* insulates the manufacturing floor from variations in customer demand. *Safety stock* insulates the customer from your internal situations, such as machine failure or absenteeism. (See Figure 1-5.)

As you read this, you may be asking yourself why anyone would recommend building inventory when one of the goals of lean manufacturing is to reduce or eliminate inventory. The answer to this question is that establishing buffer and safety stocks allows you to meet demand without requiring overtime over the short-term; it is a compromise you make as you move toward your ideal state. As your customer demand becomes more stable and you improve your internal efficiencies, your

---

**Buffer and Safety Stocks**

**Buffer Inventory**    Finished goods available to meet customer demand when customer ordering patterns vary.

**Safety Inventory**    Finished goods available to meet customer demand when internal constraints or inefficiencies disrupt process flow.

*Note:* These inventories should be stored and tracked separately. They exist for two distinct reasons.

---

**Figure 1-5.** Definitions of Buffer and Safety Stocks

buffer and safety stock inventories should be continually reviewed, reduced, and eventually eliminated.

## Buffer Stock

An inventory of finished goods, buffer stock protects the plant against dramatic customer fluctuation. The amount of buffer stock should be based on the volatility of your customer orders over a six- to eight-week period of time.

Ideally, you should produce the same amount of product every day and let the buffer stock absorb the shock of variation in demand—up or down. Your future state operations should be flexible enough to handle a 10 percent variation above normal production. (Note that this 10 percent level is not absolute; your individual circumstances will dictate how you will handle variation in demand.) Fluctuations above 10 percent are absorbed by buffer stock, which can be used when you are unable or unwilling to work overtime to meet a sharp increase in customer demand.

Buffer stock is generally self-rotating. What is withdrawn today will be replaced tomorrow. This said, however, it is best to set up a permanent rotation schedule. To calculate buffer stock, follow these steps:

1. Evaluate customer orders over a six- to eight-week period to determine variation in customer demand. (This time frame can be adjusted as needed to reflect your particular circumstances.)

2. Determine the average daily demand by dividing the total demand in units by the number of days that you used in your calculation.

3. Set the buffer at the highest spike above the average daily demand during that period. If the spike occurs over several days, you will have to use the cumulative difference between the average and the spike over the higher period.

4. You must continuously monitor customer activity so you can adjust the buffer inventory as needed to support demand.

### CALCULATING BUFFER STOCK AT SLMS – TWO EXAMPLES

#### Case 1

SLMS checked DC Mfg.'s usage for the month of April (see the partial data in Figure 1-6) and determined that the average daily demand of blue tops was 580 units. The history showed that the biggest spike in customer requirements during the period was 80 units. Therefore, SLMS set the buffer at 80 units of blue tops.

**SLMS Molding, Inc.**

## Calculation of Buffer Stock

*Case 1*

**BLUE TOP**

| April | shipped | buffer |      |
|-------|---------|--------|------|
| 1     | 660     | 80     | **   |
| 2     | 500     |        |      |
| 3     | 560     |        |      |
| 4     | 580     |        |      |
| 5     | 600     | 20     |      |
| 8     | 580     |        |      |
| 9     | 560     |        |      |
| 10    | 620     | 40     |      |
| 11    | 540     |        |      |
| 12    | 600     | 20     |      |

Avg. daily withdrawal is 580 units of Blue Tops.

**660 − 580 = 80
Buffer should be set at 80 units.

History has shown that the biggest spike in customer requirements for month of April is 80 units, i.e., the average daily withdrawal is 580 units. The most the customer has taken above that is 80 units. Therefore, the buffer will be set at 80.

Figure 1-6. Case 1—SLMS Buffer Stock Calculation (A)

SLMS still only makes 580 blue tops daily. On days when the customer orders more, it makes up the difference by pulling from buffer stock. For example, on May 15, the customer took 660 blue tops: 580 from daily production and 80 from buffer stock. The following day, the customer only took 500 units, and 80 units went back to buffer stock. Because SLMS's calculations revealed that demand above daily average never exceeded one or two days in a row, setting the buffer at 80 provided an adequate cushion. The key is to take a period of time that will give you a reasonable picture of what has happened in the past so that you can calculate short-term future anticipated need.

### Case 2

Suppose, however, that SLMS discovered that average daily demand of blue tops during the baseline month was 580 units, with a spike occurring over a four-day period (see Figure 1-7). To accommodate the spike, SLMS set the buffer at 160 units: the total amount exceeding 580 units for the four-day period. Since the spike lasted more than a day or two, SLMS's buffer stock had to be recalculated to accommodate the number of days that consumption surpassed the average until it returned to the average or below.

**SLMS Molding, Inc.**

# Calculation of Buffer Stock

*Case 2*

**BLUE TOP**

| April | shipped | buffer | |
|-------|---------|--------|------|
| 1 | 660 | 80 | * |
| 2 | 620 | 40 | ** |
| 3 | 600 | 20 | *** |
| 4 | 600 | 20 | **** |
| 5 | 580 | | |
| 8 | 500 | | |
| 9 | 540 | | |
| 10 | 580 | | |
| 11 | 580 | | |
| 12 | 520 | | |

Avg. daily withdrawal is 580 units of Blue Tops.

****Buffer should be set at 160 units.

History has shown that the biggest spike for month of April has occurred over a 4-day period.

Customer ordered more than 580 units several days in a row. The total for those 4 days (160 units) is where you need to set the buffer level.

Figure 1-7. Case 2—SLMS Buffer Stock Calculation (B)

### CALCULATING BUFFER STOCK AT SLMS (continued)

#### Rotation Schedule

In each case, SLMS decided to use a two-week rotation schedule. To standardize rotation, SLMS automatically rotated buffer stock on the 5th and 20th day of the month, even if buffer had been added the day before.

## Safety Stock

An inventory of finished goods, safety stock protects the customer against your internal constraints, e.g., a mechanical failure in your manufacturing system, a labor shortage, training, etc. It is kept separate from buffer stock.

Despite your efforts to continuously make your processes more and more capable, failures will occur. You cannot put the customer at risk when something goes awry, so you must set aside safety stock. The amount of safety stock should be based on your determination of the capability of the equipment in your process to support the nor-

### SAFETY STOCK AT SLMS

To calculate appropriate safety stock levels, SLMS considered various factors, including the lead times for obtaining normal repair parts for fixtures, tools, and machines. Short of a catastrophic failure, the company determined that it could fix anything in the plant within eight hours. It settled on a lead time of eight hours, or one shift. Therefore, it set the safety stock level for blue tops at 280, which equals approximately one-half of the daily average withdrawal of 580 units. (SLMS selected a quantity of 280 rather than 290, exactly half the daily average, because 280 divides evenly by the pack quantity of 20 units.)

SLMS then set up its rotation plan for safety stock to alternate with the rotation of buffer stock. Each week, the company rotated either safety or buffer stock. On the 15th and 30th, material handlers took customer orders to the safety stock area. As they did when rotating buffer inventory, they pulled finished goods matching a customer order and moved the goods to the shipping lanes.

mal daily demand of the customer. Remember that this is emergency stock. As you improve your process capability and total productive maintenance (TPM), you must reduce safety stock levels accordingly.

If you withdraw items from safety stock, you will most likely have to work overtime to replace them. Factors that should be considered in determining the amount of safety stock you need may include lead time for normal repair parts, fixtures, tools, machines, etc. A suggested quantity would be the amount of product you produce in eight hours. If you maintain your equipment, the need for drawing from safety stock will be minimal. To calculate safety stock levels, determine what you will require to support the normal daily demand of the customer if you have a system failure.

It is a good idea to alternate safety stock rotation with buffer stock rotation. For instance, every two weeks, instead of shipping directly from the line, ship the safety stock to the customer and replenish the safety stock with parts from the line.

## Log System

Logs must be kept to note the usage of both buffer and safety stocks. These logs should be posted at storage locations and filled out each time product is removed from either stock. Logs should be turned in daily, at a specified time, to the plant manager or other person monitoring the production process. The use of buffer and safety stocks is a way to measure production status, and the log system is the communication system that alerts managers to problems that need to be corrected or conditions that need immediate response.

Color coding can be used to distinguish buffer stocks from safety stocks. Withdrawal kanbans, discussed in Chapter 4, can be similarly color coded so that everyone knows whether customer demand or internal failure has caused withdrawal from the buffer or safety stock and what needs to be replenished.

The guidelines below can be used to create buffer and safety stock withdrawal logs. Enter the following information:

1. The department where the log is used
2. The date the material is withdrawn
3. The shift during which the product is removed
4. The part name or number of the product removed from the buffer stock
5. The amount of product removed (e.g., four boxes)
6. The reason the product was removed (see examples in Figure 1-8)
7. The signature of the person who removed the stock

8. The person who receives the log sheet (e.g., the plant manager)

9. What time the sheet is turned in

---

### Reasons for Stock Withdrawal

When you fill in this information, be as specific as possible. Here are some examples:

**From Buffer Stock**
- Customer called at last second requesting additional parts
- Customer lost product, needed more

**From Safety Stock**
- Tool 1234 broke an ejector pin
- Press 4 down 3 hours due to electrical problems

---

Figure 1-8. Reasons for Stock Withdrawal

## Buffer Stock Withdrawal Log

When you withdraw buffer stock, record it in the buffer stock withdrawal log. This gives you a history of the variation in demand. (See the sample buffer stock withdrawal log page for SLMS in Figure 1-9.) Under most circumstances, you would not

### SLMS Molding, Inc.
### Strut Department
Daily Buffer Stock Withdrawal Log

Date:  7/11

| Shift | Part Name / # | Quantity | Reason | Signature |
|-------|---------------|----------|--------|-----------|
| 2 | Green Top | 2 | Customer demand does fluctuate | T. L. |
| | | | | |
| | | | | |
| | | | | |
| | | | | |
| | | | | |
| | | | | |
| | | | | |
| | | | | |
| | | | | |
| | | | | |

Turn log sheet in to **Product Control** each day by **3:00 PM**

If no withdrawals have been made write NONE across the sheet and turn it in.

Figure 1-9. SLMS Completed Daily Buffer Stock Withdrawal Log

have more than one day of buffer in inventory; but *you must continuously watch for trends in customer volatility and adjust buffer stock as necessary.* The log provides the information you need to do this; for this reason, it should be posted where the buffer stock is stored.

### Daily Safety Stock Withdrawal Log

When a system fails, the root cause must be found and eliminated. At a minimum, countermeasures must be put in place. Often, a simple log is the standardizing tool that alerts management that a problem needs attention. (See the sample buffer stock withdrawal log page for SLMS in Figure 1-10.)

The general manager or the highest ranking manager at the facility must sign the log to release safety stock for use. While this ensures that safety stock will not be withdrawn for the wrong reasons, it also promotes system improvement: There is nothing more likely to induce root cause investigations than the boss making a few pre-dawn

**SLMS Molding, Inc.**

## Strut Department

Daily Safety Stock Withdrawal Log

Date: 8/11

| Shift | Part Name / # | Quantity | Reason | Signature |
|---|---|---|---|---|
| 2 | Green Top | 4 | Paint line breakdown | D. T. |
|  |  |  |  |  |
|  |  |  |  |  |
|  |  |  |  |  |
|  |  |  |  |  |
|  |  |  |  |  |
|  |  |  |  |  |
|  |  |  |  |  |
|  |  |  |  |  |
|  |  |  |  |  |
|  |  |  |  |  |
|  |  |  |  |  |
|  |  |  |  |  |

Turn log sheet in to **Shift Supervisor** each day by **3:00 PM**

If no withdrawals have been made write NONE across the sheet and turn it in.

**Figure 1-10.** SLMS Completed Daily Safety Stock Withdrawal Log

drives to sign emergency safety stock withdrawal log entries. (At SLMS, the general manager keeps the key to the safety stock cage. If he gets a 3:00 A.M. call to drive in to release safety stock, he expects to see a team already working on the problem when he walks in.)

## Moving On

Now that you have a basic understanding of customer demand, it is time to review your own operations through self-evaluation. You will determine your capabilities to meet this demand in relation to labor, material management, and equipment and process capability. Chapter 2 examines practical ways to accomplish things and includes case studies showing how SLMS handled the discovery process in each of these areas and then applied the resulting knowledge to its future state value stream.

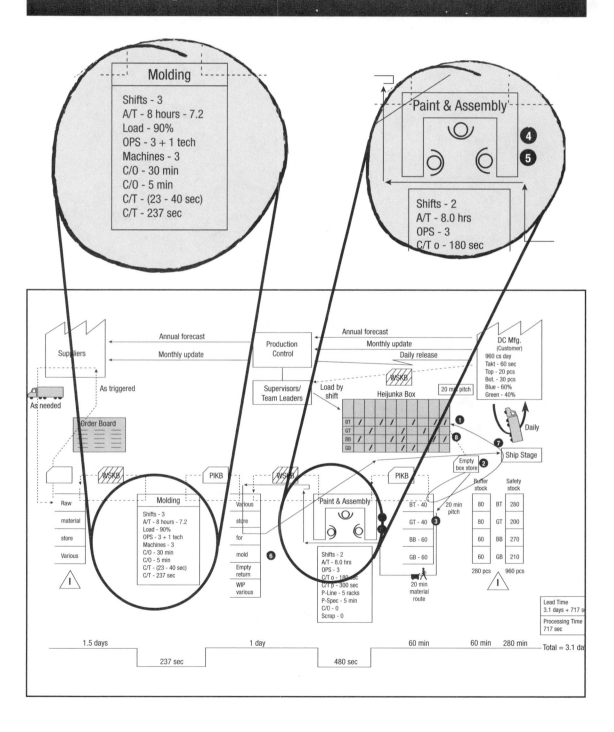

**Molding**

Shifts - 3
A/T - 8 hours - 7.2
Load - 90%
OPS - 3 + 1 tech
Machines - 3
C/O - 30 min
C/O - 5 min
C/T - (23 - 40 sec)
C/T - 237 sec

**Paint & Assembly**

Shifts - 2
A/T - 8.0 hrs
OPS - 3
C/T o - 180 sec

Suppliers

Annual forecast
Monthly update

Production Control

Annual forecast
Monthly update
Daily release

As triggered

As needed

Order Board

WSKB

Supervisors/
Team Leaders

Load by
shift

WSKB

Heijunka Box

20 min pitch

DC Mfg.
(Customer)
960 cs day
Takt - 60 sec
Top - 20 pcs
Bot. - 30 pcs
Blue - 60%
Green - 40%

BT /
GT /
BB /
GB /

Daily

Ship Stage

Empty
box store

20 min
pitch

WSKB

PIKB

WSKB

PIKB

Raw

material

store

Various

**Molding**

Shifts - 3
A/T - 8 hours - 7.2
Load - 90%
OPS - 3 + 1 tech
Machines - 3
C/O - 30 min
C/O - 5 min
C/T - (23 - 40 sec)
C/T - 237 sec

Various

store

for

mold

Empty
return

WIP
various

**Paint & Assembly**

Shifts - 2
A/T - 8.0 hrs
OPS - 3
C/T o - 180 sec
C/T p - 300 sec
P-Line - 5 racks
P-Spec - 5 min
C/O - 0
Scrap - 0

BT - 40

GT - 40

BB - 60

GB - 60

20 min
material
route

Buffer
stock

80
80
60
60

280 pcs

Safety
stock

BT  280
GT  200
BB  270
GB  210

960 pcs

Lead Time
3.1 days + 717 s

Processing Time
717 sec

1.5 days

237 sec

1 day

480 sec

60 min    60 min    280 min

Total = 3.1 da

# Chapter 2. Self-evaluation

The next step in stabilizing production is to evaluate your own operations. You have already begun your self-evaluation by creating your safety stock, but there is much more to know about your own operations before you can shift your production process to a pull system and go lean. Self-evaluation includes looking at five aspects of your operation:

1. Determining and verifying operator cycle times
2. Balancing the line
3. Calculating machine capacity
4. Assessing process capability
5. Calculating WIP inventory

## Operator Cycle Time

Once you understand customer demand, you are almost ready to design and staff an assembly operation that will meet demand successfully and efficiently. When you created your value stream maps, you probably took some simple cycle time measurements of the process steps to complete the maps quickly. At this point, as you move toward a future state cell that works the way you want it to work, you must delve more deeply into each step to evaluate your operation. This can only be done on the shop floor.

Cycle time evaluation is a straightforward process that uses traditional time study methods to obtain operator cycle times and process cycle times, but there is a difference between the methodologies. Instead of balancing labor to the capacity of the equipment, as traditional time studies do, a lean organization balances labor to customer demand. The *operator cycle time worksheet* is a tool to help you collect current time data about the process.

### Cycle Time Work Sheet

Cycle time work sheets (see Figures 2-1a and 2-1b) are used to evaluate each element of each operation based on the current condition of an operation in terms of time. A

**SLMS Molding, Inc.**

**Cycle Time Worksheet**

INSTRUCTIONS

| | | |
|---|---|---|
| 1. | Operation Name | Operation Name |
| 2. | Oper. No. | Operator Number |
| 3. | P/N | Part Number |
| 4. | Date | Date |
| 5. | By | Name of person who did time study |
| 6. | Element No. | Element Number |
| 7. | Description | Description of element (i.e. insert vanes) |
| 8. | Sample Times | Time it takes to do the element |
| 9. | Most Freq. | Out of 10 cycles, the number that occurs most frequently |
| 10. | HI | The high number out of the 10 sample times |
| 11. | LOW REPEAT | The low repeatable number out of the 10 sample times |
| 12. | Total Cycle Time | Total cycle time of operation (add most freq. elements) |
| 13. | Total HI Time | Total of high times |
| 14. | Total LOW Time | Total of low repeatable times |

**Figure 2-1a.** Cycle Time Worksheet Instructions

cycle time worksheet gives you the information you need to create an operator balance chart and allows you to study your current situation to see how balanced your line really is.

## How to Collect Data for the Cycle Time Worksheet

To collect cycle time data, the supervisor, with assistance from the manufacturing engineer or the equivalent function at your facility, studies the process on the floor, lists all the work elements, and determines the time required for each element (e.g., pick up part, walk, start machine, etc.). Showing up on the shop floor with a clipboard and pencil without notice does not work very well. The supervisor and ME must tell the operators ahead of time what they will be measuring and why.

Operators must understand that this exercise is about eliminating waste, not reducing headcount. They must also know that they will have a chance to operate the new cell and offer improvement ideas. By inviting worker participation, the company builds

## Standard Operations

**Cycle Time Worksheet**

Operation Name: ①

Oper. No.: ②    P/N: ③

Date: ④

By: ⑤

| Element No. ⑥ | Description ⑦ | Sample Times | | | | | | | | | | Most Freq. | HI | Low Repeat |
|---|---|---|---|---|---|---|---|---|---|---|---|---|---|---|
| | | 1 | 2 | 3 | 4 | 5 ⑧ | 6 | 7 | 8 | 9 | 10 | ⑨ | ⑩ | ⑪ |
| | | | | | | | | | | | | | | |
| | | | | | | | | | | | | | | |
| **Total Cycle Time** | | | | | | | | | | | | ⑫ | ⑬ | ⑭ |

*Note*: Most frequent will be the starting point for the Future State Assembly Operation.

Figure 2-1b. Operator Cycle Time Worksheet

the base from which it hopes to get greater involvement, which will ultimately improve quality of life on the shop floor and the company's competitive edge.

You must also plan ahead for the people who will be freed by the leaner, more productive future state value stream. Reassign them to other areas or to kaizen teams or to a function established for driving the lean transition process. Some companies call this function a kaizen promotion office.

Once workers have been apprised of the reasons for the exercise and assured that the ensuing changes will lead to improvements in their work routines, you are ready to begin gathering the data you need. Tools and guidelines for this process are listed below:

### Tools required

- Cycle time worksheet
- Video camera with a timer that will show seconds on screen

### Instructions

1. Videotape the process. Someone can tape the job at the same time others are timing the elements.

2. Time each element for at least 10 cycles or long enough to give you accurate information on the floor. Time one element at a time—**do not use standard times,** because these will give you "ballpark" rather than the specific data you need.

3. Review the tape to confirm that all of the elements have been identified.

4. If the process runs on more than one shift, **time all shifts**.

5. For each element, record the
   a. HI (the highest time element).
   b. LOW REPEATABLE (the lowest repeatable time element).
      **Note:** Do not count a single incidence of lowest time. Something unrepeatable might have occurred for the operator to achieve that time. The *lowest repeatable time* is the lowest time observed more than once.
   c. MOST FREQUENT (the most frequent time element observed during the 10 cycles).

6. Total each column.

7. Use MOST FREQUENT as a baseline from which to improve each work element.

8. Use LOW REPEATABLE as a realistic target for each element. Find out if the operator did something different during those cycles that led to the low time. Use the video to determine exactly what was done differently to make those cycles shorter.

9. Use HI to find out what occurred during that cycle to cause a spike. There is probably a recurring problem that must be solved so it does not continue to disrupt the future state system or cause it to fail completely. Again, refer to the video to identify what happened.

10. Add the cycle times of all the work elements to determine the total cycle time required to build the product.

In the next section, you will divide the total cycle time by the takt time to determine how many operators you need in the future state process. First, look at the SLMS cycle time worksheet and the data collected for evaluating cycle time (see Figures 2-2 and 2-3). Please note that this information is the foundation for the operator instruction sheet, which is covered in Chapter 4.

## Assembly Line Labor Balancing

One of the essential tasks in creating a pull system is to determine how best to distribute work elements (operations) in the value stream to meet takt time. This task is called **line balancing**.

Every production process, or value stream, functions like a river. Materials should flow in factories just as water flows in a river, but without any boulders or rapids. Typically, some operations take longer than others, leaving operators with nothing to do while they wait for the next part. On the other hand, some operations may require more than one operator. To try to attain the ideal state of no waiting and optimal use of personnel, use line balancing based on takt time. (See Figure 2-4.)

### Operator Balance Chart

Line balancing begins with an analysis of your current state. The best tool to perform this task is an operator balance chart. An operator balance chart gives you a visual representation of the current condition. It can then be used to determine how to balance work on the line. There are several steps to creating an operator balance chart and then determining the best solution to balancing the line to takt time.

**Standard Operations**

**Cycle Time Worksheet**

Operation Name:  Bottom Support Arm

Oper. No.: 32

Date: 5/1

By: T. L.

P/N: _____

| Element No. | Description | Sample Times | | | | | | | | | | Most Freq. | HI | Low Repeat |
|---|---|---|---|---|---|---|---|---|---|---|---|---|---|---|
| | | 1 | 2 | 3 | 4 | 5 | 6 | 7 | 8 | 9 | 10 | | | |
| 1 | Strut to Arm | 28 | 26 | 29 | 28 | 28 | 26 | 28 | 32 | 28 | 29 | 28 | 32 | 26 |
| 2 | Strut/Arm to Base | 18 | 18 | 16 | 19 | 20 | 18 | 18 | 19 | 16 | 18 | 18 | 20 | 16 |
| | | | | | | | | | | | | | | |
| | | | | | | | | | | | | | | |
| | | | | | | | | | | | | | | |
| | | | | | | | | | | | | | | |
| | | | | | | | | | | | | | | |
| | | | | | | | | | | | | | | |
| | | | | | | | | | | | | | | |
| | | | | | | | | | | | | | | |
| | | | | | | | | | | | | | | |
| | | | | | | | | | | | | | | |
| | | | | | | | | | | | | | | |
| | | | | | | | | | | | | | | |
| | **Total Cycle Time** | | | | | | | | | | | | | |

*Note:* Most frequent will be the starting point for the Future State Assembly Operation.

Figure 2-2. SLMS Cycle Time Worksheet, Partially Completed.

## Observed Assembly Times

**Bottom**
*Work elements and time*

| | |
|---|---|
| Strut to Arm | 28 seconds |
| Strut/Arm to Base | 18 seconds |
| Strut/Arm/Base to Cap | 14 seconds |
| Add Clip | 14 seconds |
| Inspect | 8 seconds |
| Pack | 4 seconds |
| **Total** | **86 seconds** |

**Top**
*Work elements and time*

| | |
|---|---|
| Side to Base | 26 seconds |
| Side/Base to Leg | 24 seconds |
| Side/Base/Leg to Cap | 10 seconds |
| Add Clip | 10 seconds |
| Inspect | 8 seconds |
| Pack | 4 seconds |
| **Total** | **82 seconds** |

**Total cycle time to build product:**

| | |
|---|---|
| Bottom | 86 seconds |
| Top | 82 seconds |
| Paint | 12 seconds |
| | **168 seconds** |

**Figure 2-3.** Cycle Time Data for Paint and Assembly Operations at SLMS

## Line or Labor Balancing

Line balancing is the process by which you evenly distribute the work elements within a value stream in order to meet takt time.

**Figure 2-4.** Definition of Line Balancing

### *Review cycle times and determine how many operators are needed*

1. Review the information gathered from all the cycle time worksheets, including cycle times and number of operators for each operation. At SLMS, the assembly operation consists of 13 distinct operations done by 4 operators in each shift. (See Figure 2-3 for the SLMS example.) Included in this review was the cycle time it took for an operator to paint the top and bottom caps, though the time for the painting is not included in the figure.

2. Next, determine the number of operators needed by dividing total product cycle time by takt time. (See Figure 2-5.)

**SLMS Top/Bottom Assembly**

Takt time = 60 seconds

| Element/Desc. | Time (sec.) | Element/Desc. | Time (sec.) |
|---|---|---|---|
| 1 Strut to Arm | 28 | 1 Side to Base | 26 |
| 2 Strut/Arm to Base | 18 | 2 Side/Base to Leg | 24 |
| 3 Strut/Arm/Base to Cap | 14 | 3 Side/Base/Leg to Cap | 10 |
| 4 Add Clip | 14 | 4 Add Clip | 10 |
| 5 Inspect | 8 | 5 Inspect | 8 |
| 6 Pack | 4 | 6 Pack | 4 |
| **Total** | **86** | **Total** | **82** |

$$\text{\# operators needed} = \frac{168 \text{ sec. (cycle time)}}{60 \text{ sec. (takt time)}} = 2.8 \text{ operators}$$

Conclusion: Staff line with 3 operators and continue to Kaizen

**Figure 2-5.** Operator Cycle Times and Calculation of Number of Operators Needed

### Create the Operator Balance Chart—Current State

Make the chart with a bar for each operator following the steps listed below. Do not use computer programs that claim to perform these functions automatically.

1. Write the program name or part name on a wall chart, flip chart paper, or other large sheet. Large cardboard or poster board works well, too. First, draw a vertical axis on the left to represent time in seconds. Segment it with a tick mark every 5 or 10 seconds, or whatever interval is appropriate for your takt time. Draw a horizontal line along the bottom and another colored horizontal line across the top of the board at the takt time point.

2. Write the name of each work element on a sticky note, i.e., strut to arm, or activate fixture, or turn on machine. Make a separate sticky note for each work element.

3. Using data from the cycle time work sheet, write in seconds the **most frequent** and the **low repeatable** times.

4. Cut the paper you make for each work element to represent proportionally the time each work element represents, i.e., one inch of paper equals ten seconds. Use the **most frequent** times for sizing the paper. Thus, in the example below the most frequent time of 28–26 seconds for the strut to arm operation produces a note 2.8 inches long. (See Figure 2-6.)

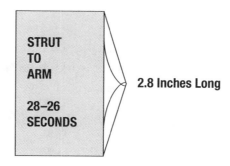

**Figure 2-6.** Work Element Symbol for the Operator Balance Chart

5. Use a different color sticky note for inspection times to clearly distinguish this element from the others.

6. Place the work element sticky notes end-to-end vertically for each operator on the wall chart you prepared in step 1. The operator bars should stack vertically from the base horizontal line upwards toward the colored takt time line. If you have four operators, you will have four columns of sticky notes stacked side by side in vertical columns. (See Figure 2-7.)

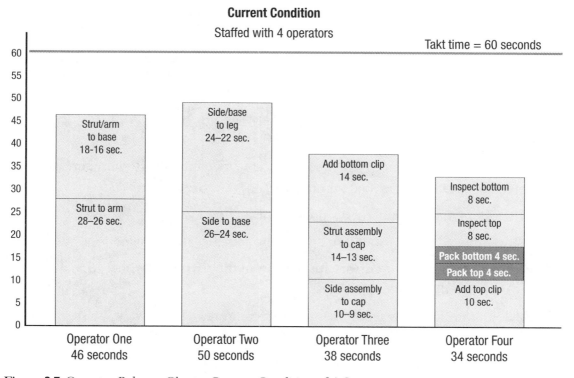

**Figure 2-7.** Operator Balance Chart—Current Condition of 4 Operators

## Balance the work

To balance the work, move the elements (the sticky notes) around on the chart, so that the work is balanced among operators working to takt time while maintaining the flow of the operation. The ideal situation is to have every operator working at takt time (see Figure 2-8).

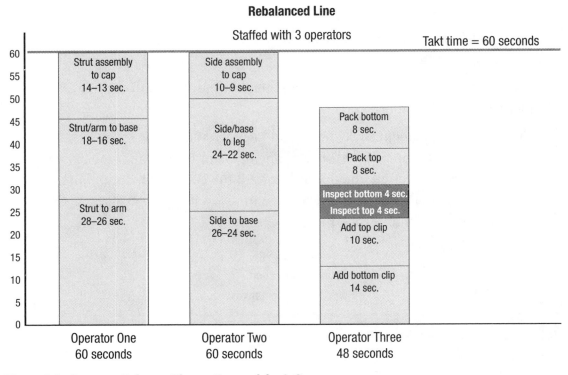

**Figure 2-8.** Operator Balance Chart—Proposal for 3 Operators

1. Use reasonable judgment when combining work elements. Remember, flow comes first. Do not overload an operator.

2. Move elements to maintain a smooth process flow.

3. Incorporate additional walk time with new activities for operator.

4. Please allow time for a **cursory inspection** of the part. Remember to make this sticky note a different color.

5. Review your design to see if one operator could reasonably walk the steps that you have created and still produce a part within takt.

6. Critique the design with a three-stage process: The lean team should evaluate the design first, then the supervisor, finally the operator.

## Operator Balance Chart—Proposal for 3 Operators

A 2.8-operator requirement creates a problem. It means that there is not enough work to occupy three workers fully, but you are still paying for that time. This situation, however, provides an opportunity to set an improvement target: to eliminate enough waste in the line so that only two operators are needed. A progressively lean process might solve this problem by absorbing the third operation into the first two operations, but there could be other solutions. The ideal situation is to have every operator working at takt time.

At SLMS, the initial operator balance chart showed that the assembly operation could be run with 3 operators. A second option that SLMS considered and ultimately implemented was to create a paint/assembly cell, merge the operations and use three operators in the cell each shift. The example shown in Figure 2-9 demonstrates the value of this process. Innovations emerge as you study your operations this closely and continually consider how to improve in the direction of takt time performance.

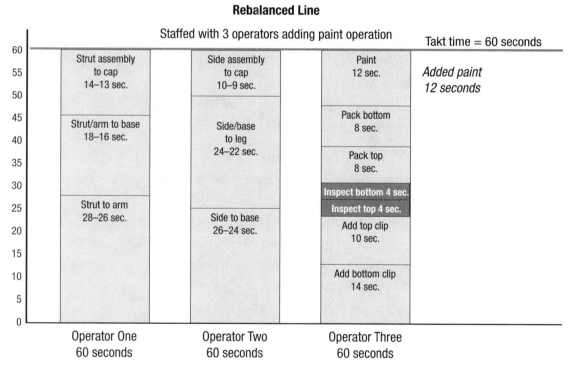

**Figure 2-9.** Operator Balance Chart—Proposal for Paint/Assembly Cell with 3 Operators

SLMS reviewed the paint specifications and determined that the paint flash off, drying time, and cool down took a total of 5 minutes. Armed with this information, their paint engineer, with the assistance of an operator, was able to prototype a much smaller paint system that had 6 racks versus the 120 on the original monument paint line. It worked, and this allowed SLMS to balance the 12 seconds of painting time (shown on the original current state map) in with the assembly operation.

Now you have a target. However, the question still remains: *How* are three future state operators going to complete their work in the targeted time? The best response to this question is standardized work, which will be discussed in Chapter 4.

## Machine Balance in Relation to Capacity, Demand, and Labor

In lean production, the workers and the machines must all be balanced to takt, or moving in that direction to whatever extent possible. In traditional production environments *full work* describes a condition when all machines are working at capacity or just "staying busy." This has been understood to be the most cost-effective use of capital equipment. In direct contrast to this century-old notion, in a lean environment where pull production drives the plant in response to actual customer orders, machines may actually be more cost-effective when they are idle at times.

This is meant to be a controversial comment. It is intended to make you think carefully about the principle behind pull production—*that you lose more money by creating inventory than you do by pacing the production of people AND machines to the pace of customer demand. In a lean environment, full work means the condition when all machines and people are working to takt time.*

Understanding your machine capacity and how to balance it to support takt time is critical and involves several steps. First, you determine the demand that is placed on your capital equipment by your customer base, and then you organize the machine operations just as you did with the operator work elements so that machine capacity is synchronized to the overall pace of production. As you work through the steps of this process, you will begin to understand the waste involved in working your equipment at full capacity instead of to takt time. The following section provides general information on how to evaluate your capacity.

*Evaluating machine capacity*

1. Gather data on each machine, including how it is scheduled, staffing requirements, changeover times, uptime, scrap, and actual cycle times. Remember: Do not use standard times!

2. Make a list of tools that will run in each machine. A key action or change is to dedicate tools to specific presses or machines. This may sound unreasonable or counterintuitive, but is essential for balancing your available time to demand.

3. Get an annual forecast of product volume for each product. (You gathered this information on the customer evaluation form in Chapter 1.)

4. Determine your available time. (In the SLMS case study available time was 90 percent of true time, based on the history of planned and unplanned down time. See Figure 2-10.)

---

### SLMS Molding, Inc.
### Molding Operations

| | |
|---|---|
| Available molding time: | 3 shifts |
| | 8.0 hours available per shift (relieve for breaks) |
| Standard time is: | 240 days per year |
| | 24 hours per day (=5,760 hours per year) |
| | @90% = 5,184 available production hours per year |
| Molding staffing: | 9 machine operators—3 per shift |
| | 3 machines being utilized for this product family |
| | 1 technician per shift |
| | 1st shift technician also does paint changeovers |
| Changeover time for mold: | 2 hours |
| Changeover time for color: | 15 minutes |

- Changeover time is measured from last good part of previous run to first good part of new run.

### Tooling

Supplied by the customer: You must use virgin material. All tools are hot-runner.

| Tool Number | Part Desc. | Tool Desc. | Press Size | Total Cycle | Oper. Time | Part Wt. | Material |
|---|---|---|---|---|---|---|---|
| **Top** | | | | | | | |
| S98-007 | Arm | 1 cavity | 300 ton | 30 sec | 8 sec | 4 oz. | PP |
| S98-008 | Base | 1 cavity | 200 ton | 34 sec | 8 sec | 5 oz. | ABS |
| S98-009 | Strut | 1 cavity | 350 ton | 38 sec | 8 sec | 4 oz. | PP |
| S98-010 | Cap | 1 cavity | 200 ton | 23 sec | 8 sec | 1.5 oz. | ABS |
| **Bottom** | | | | | | | |
| S98-011 | Side | 1 cavity | 300 ton | 24 sec | 8 sec | 3 oz. | ABS |
| S98-012 | Base | 1 cavity | 350 ton | 40 sec | 8 sec | 4 oz. | ABS |
| S98-013 | Leg | 1 cavity | 300 ton | 25 sec | 8 sec | 1 oz. | ABS |
| S98-014 | Cap | 1 cavity | 200 ton | 23 sec | 8 sec | 1.5 oz. | ABS |

Figure 2-10. SLMS Machine Data

5. Calculate the run minutes/day for each tool based on the following formulas:

   *Step 1:* Pieces/day = Annual volume *divided* by number of days/year. Normally, this can typically be calculated using the number of operating days, generally 240 working days per year.

   For SLMS Tool #SA98-010:

   Pieces/day = 230,400 (annual volume) ÷ 240 days = 960 pieces

   *Step 2:* Run seconds/day = Pieces/day multiplied by the cycle time for the tool.

   For SLMS Tool #SA98-010:

   Run seconds/day = 960 pieces/day × 23 second cycle time = 22,080 seconds

   *Step 3:* Run minutes/day = Run seconds/day multiplied by 60 seconds per minute.

   For SLMS Tool #SA98-010:

   Run minutes/day = 22,080 seconds/day ÷ 60 seconds/minute = 368 minutes

   Repeat steps 1 to 3 for each tool.

6. In addition to run times, determine and allow for:

   • Tool change history

   • Material change history

   • Part reject history, all inclusive: machine, secondary operations, customer, other

7. Make a bar chart for each machine operation.

   Just as you did for operators, make a chart of your machine operations on a wallboard or flip chart. Follow these steps.

   *Step 1:* Write the tool or product number and run times (in minutes/day) on a sticky note. Use one sticky note for each tool or product number.

   Cut the length of the sticky note to coincide with the required number of run minutes. Scale: 1 inch = 100 run minutes.

   Example: If run minutes = 368 minutes/day, cut sticky note to 3.68 inches (see Figure 2-11).

   Do this for run times, tool/product change times, color change times, and rejects (converted to run minutes per day). Use different color sticky notes for run time, tool/part change time, color change time, and rejects to maintain the visual effect of this process.

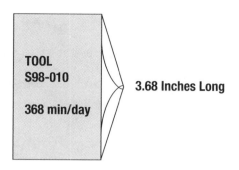

**Figure 2-11.** Work Element Symbol for Machine Balance Chart

*Step 2:* Make a bar chart for each machine.

For each machine, place sticky notes end-to-end.

Determine minutes available. One shift would be 480 minutes, two would be 960, and three would be 1,440.

This creates a visual aid for machine loading (see Figure 2-12).

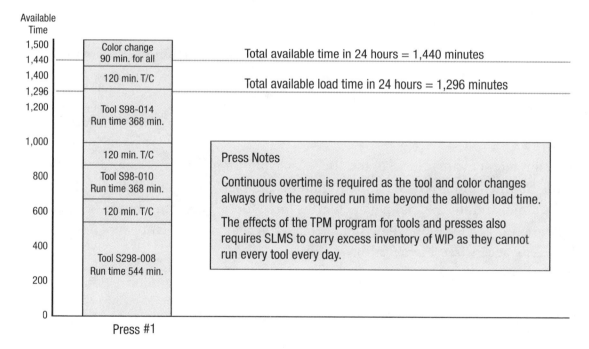

**Figure 2-12.** Machine Capacity Balancing Chart—Current

*Step 3:* Balance the machine load by moving the sticky notes around from machine to machine as you did with the operator balance chart. When only one machine is involved, as with the example in Figures 2-12 and 2-13, balancing can be achieved by reductions in changeover times, and other improvements.

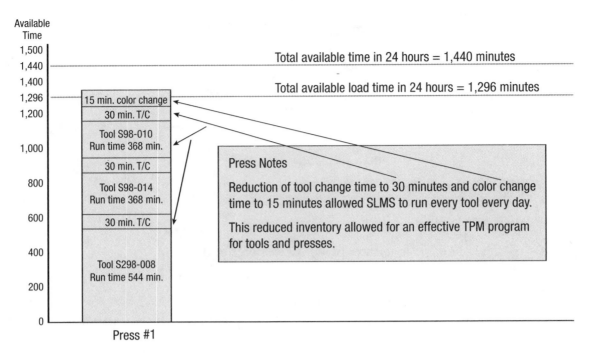

**Figure 2-13.** Machine Capacity Balancing Chart—After Improvement

> **Note:** When changing tools or products between machines, check with the process engineer and/or supervisors to make sure there will be no problems with making such a change.

8. Create machine cycle time summary forms for each press/machine.

Visual references are critical to the success of your program. The Machine Cycle Time Summary for Press/Machine should be completed to show what tools call that press home and the general parameters for those tools. This form should be displayed on the press at a location where the operator and the team leader or supervisor can have easy access (see Figure 2-14).

The machine cycle time summary form contains the following information:

| | |
|---|---|
| Machine | The Machine Number and size |
| Tool # | The tools that call this press home |
| Part # | The part number or numbers associated with that tool |
| Description | The description of the product |
| Container Size | The size of the container the parts should go in |
| Pieces per container | The quantity of parts to be placed into the container |
| Tool Cycle | The part-to-part cycle of the tool |

### SLMS Molding, Inc.
### Cycle Time Summary Per Press/Machine
Press # _____

| Tool # | Part # | Description | Cont. Size | Pcs/ Cont. | Tool Cycle (sec.) | Oper. Cycle (sec.) | Wait Time |
|--------|--------|-------------|-----------|-----------|-------------------|--------------------|-----------|
|        |        |             |           |           |                   |                    |           |
|        |        |             |           |           |                   |                    |           |
|        |        |             |           |           |                   |                    |           |
|        |        |             |           |           |                   |                    |           |
|        |        |             |           |           |                   |                    |           |
|        |        |             |           |           |                   |                    |           |
|        |        |             |           |           |                   |                    |           |
|        |        |             |           |           |                   |                    |           |
|        |        |             |           |           |                   |                    |           |
|        |        |             |           |           |                   |                    |           |
|        |        |             |           |           |                   |                    |           |
|        |        |             |           |           |                   |                    |           |
|        |        |             |           |           |                   |                    |           |
|        |        |             |           |           |                   |                    |           |

**Figure 2-14.** Cycle Time Summary Form

Operator Cycle        The operator time within the cycle of the tool

Wait time        The operator wait time, if any, during the cycle of the tool

The column on the chart designating operator wait time is important. If the length of this wait time permits, you can have the operator complete other tasks. For example, you may have the operator run multiple presses or do autonomous maintenance tasks on other machines.

SLMS's success using the assembly balance, prompted the company to review the labor in the press room. Figure 2-15, drawn from the SLMS case study, illustrates the detailed information in the cycle time summary that the company gathered for this purpose. By calculating the operator cycle time in relation to the press close time, it was possible to determine how many operators were needed to run the presses. In this

**SLMS Molding, Inc.**

## Cycle Time Summary Per Press/Machine

Press # 1-200 Ton

| Tool # | Part # | Description | Cont. Size | Pcs/ Cont. | Tool Cycle (sec.) | Oper. Cycle (sec.) | Wait Time |
|--------|--------|-------------|------------|------------|-------------------|--------------------|-----------|
| S98-008 | 98-008 | Top Base | A | 20 | 34 | 8 | 26 |
|  |  |  |  |  |  |  |  |
| S98-010 | 98-010 | Top Cap | A | 20 | 23 | 8 | 15 |
|  |  |  |  |  |  |  |  |
| S98-014 | 98-014 | Bottom Cap | A | 30 | 23 | 8 | 15 |
|  |  |  |  |  |  |  |  |
|  |  |  |  |  |  |  |  |
|  |  |  |  |  |  |  |  |
|  |  |  |  |  |  |  |  |
|  |  |  |  |  |  |  |  |
|  |  |  |  |  |  |  |  |
|  |  |  |  |  |  |  |  |
|  |  |  |  |  |  |  |  |
|  |  |  |  |  |  |  |  |
|  |  |  |  |  |  |  |  |

**Figure 2-15.** SLMS Machine Cycle Time Summary for Press/Machine

calculation, SLMS used the labor demand (8 seconds) in relation to available Tool Cycle Time to determine the required labor for each tool. For example, Tool S98-008:

Press Cycle time   =   34 seconds

Less Operator time   –  8 seconds part removal

           =   26 seconds close time = 26 seconds operator wait time

           8/26 = .31 operators or labor ratio

Using the highest labor ratio for all presses, SLMS saw the potential to run all presses with just one operator. This presented a perfect opportunity for a kaizen event to determine what steps might be taken to take full advantage of the possibilities suggested by the discovery.

## WIP

Once you know your machine capacity and balance it to your lean operations, you can determine the proper lot size you will need for work-in-process (WIP) inventory. WIP, in the SLMS case study, is the finished goods for the molding operation and the raw material for the assembly operation, but the identical premise holds true for all materials in a given value stream. You do not yet have the capability to change tools in zero seconds; you will have changeover time (tool and color) and other tools competing for the run time on the same machine. This is where WIP comes in, but you should try to keep WIP to a minimum. The rule of thumb is that if you never run out, you have too much WIP. Keep the following points in mind when calculating how much WIP you need:

1. When parts are for internal use, it is recommended that the lot sizes be based on pitch.

2. Pitch should be taken into consideration when determining lot size. For example, if the pitch is 20 minutes, you would not want a WIP container that holds 2 minutes worth of product. The material handler would have to supply 10 containers every round. And vice versa, if the pitch is 6 minutes, you would not want a WIP container that holds 30 minutes; you would try to reduce this number to 6, or possibly 12.

3. It is important that you locate the WIP store as close to the point of manufacture as possible. The point of manufacture is the point that produces the WIP components, not the point that uses them. For example, the point of manufacture would be a molding press; the point of use would be the assembly operation. In this example, the WIP would be stored at each respective molding press.

The next step is to determine WIP store inventory levels and container lot sizes.

### WIP Calculation

The WIP calculation is based on the machine balance, as described in the previous section on balancing capital equipment. If machine balance shows every tool can be run once every day, than you will need one day of WIP to support your daily production requirements. If every tool can be run twice per day, then half a day of WIP is all that is needed.

Hours of WIP quantity are calculated in terms of daily customer demand. If the daily customer requirement is 960 pieces/day and the WIP is set for one day's demand, then the WIP for the blue base would be set at 580 pieces for Tool S98-008. If WIP were equal to half-day demand then WIP would be 290 pieces (see Figure 2-16).

**One example:  Tool – S98-008**

| | | |
|---|---|---|
| Daily demand = | **960 pcs** | **WIP levels per color** |
| 2 colors or products | (60% – Blue) (40% – Green) | 576 (580) pieces 384 (390) pieces |
| | **Total =** | **960 pieces** |

**Note:** WIP levels are rounded up to a number divisible by the pack quantity of 20.

**Figure 2-16.** SLMS WIP Calculation

If the WIP store needs to hold one day of customer demand (i.e., run every tool once per day), each tool must run long enough to produce one day's worth of customer demand. For example, it will be 6.1 hours of machine time for Tool S98-010 (see Figure 2-17).

## Operator Balancing Machine

| Press # | Size | Tool No. | Press C/T (sec.) | Hrs/Day | Oper. C/T (sec.) | # of OPS (Labor Ratio) | |
|---|---|---|---|---|---|---|---|
| 1 | 200 T | S98-008 | 34 | 7.5 | 8 | 0.31 | |
| 1 | 200 T | S98-010 | 23 | 6.1 | 8 | 0.35 | * |
| 1 | 200 T | S98-014 | 23 | 6.1 | 8 | 0.35 | * |
| 2 | 300 T | S98-007 | 30 | 8.0 | 8 | 0.27 | |
| 2 | 300 T | S98-011 | 24 | 6.4 | 8 | 0.33 | * |
| 2 | 300 T | S98-013 | 25 | 6.7 | 8 | 0.32 | |
| 3 | 350 T | S98-009 | 38 | 10.1 | 8 | 0.21 | * |
| 3 | 350 T | S98-012 | 40 | 10.7 | 8 | 0.20 | |

Total operators required = 0.35 + 0.33 + 0.21 = 0.89) ops

*Denotes Hi operator time for each machine

**Figure 2-17.** SLMS Labor Balance for Molding Operations

**Note:** Please make sure that you understand that this is one day of customer demand, not 24 hours of machine run time. **There is a difference!**

Standard Work in Process (SWIP) stock will depend on a variety of things. You must take into consideration:

1. Tool changeover time
2. Color changeover time

3. Competing run times

4. Historical scrap rates

5. Other variables that may be unique to your process

## WIP Store Container and Storage

In addition to calculating the WIP quantity, you must determine the proper sizing of WIP containers, and how to store them.

### Per container calculation

The amount of WIP per container is based on finished goods pack quantity, pitch, and takt time. The WIP container size should divide evenly into the finished goods pack quantity and should also correspond with your takt time and pitch. For example:

If the finished goods pack quantity = 20 pieces, then the WIP container can be 1, 2, 4, 5, 10 or 20, which all divide evenly into 20.

If the takt time is 60 seconds and pitch = 20 minutes, a WIP container that holds 10 or 20 minutes worth of product is the ideal target.

A WIP container with 20 components will satisfy both requirements.

### Stack height calculation—a visual system

When storing WIP, stack height limits are used to display the height at which the containers will be stacked. When using height limits, there is no need to count the number of containers in a stack. Once the height limit is reached, the visual signal shows that the stack of containers should be pushed forward.

It is recommended that stack heights be no higher than eye level, unless you are dealing with very large items or materials. The following is an example showing the stack height calculations for two different products.

| Color | Pieces | # Containers | Height | Depth | Total |
|-------|--------|--------------|--------|-------|-------|
| Blue | 580(20) | 29 | 5 cont. | 6 cont. | 30 cont. |
| Green | 390(15) | 26 | 3 cont. | 9 cont. | 27 cont. |

The height and depth calculation will be affected by the amount of space you have to work with. In some instances, you may only be able to stack the product 4 deep. If this is the case, you have a choice to make. Either stack blue containers 6 high and 5 deep, or if this is too high (that is, greater than 54 inches), you may have to make 2 rows of blue containers. Common sense will dictate which of these is the better alternative.

*Marking height limits:*

There are two visuals that should be in place in your WIP supermarkets—the maximum limit and the replacement point; plastic chains can be used to mark these trigger points.

- RED should be used to mark the maximum limit line for inventory. The red line is simple; it is placed at the last stack of containers (if the limit is 4 containers deep, put the red line at 4 deep).

- YELLOW should be used to mark when to start replenishing the store. The yellow line is based on the time it takes to change a tool, plus some buffer. This Standard Work In Process (SWIP) stock will depend on a variety of things:

  1. If material takes 2 hours to dry, than you must take this into account when establishing the yellow line.

  2. If tool S98-010 takes 6.1 hours to run in the press, the yellow line should reflect this.

  3. You must take into consideration changeover time and competing run time of the other tools in the press. Consider that when you are running tool S98-010, you must have sufficient SWIP stock for materials created with tools S98-014 and S98-008, etc., to prevent downstream operations from running out of those materials.

  4. Use reasonable judgment on establishing these levels.

If product consistently runs out, reevaluate the yellow line; it may be set too low, not allowing enough time to react after the trigger is reached. On the other hand, the yellow line may be set too high, making you run the tool more often than the system can currently support. Be aware that once you establish the yellow lines, you may have to adjust them a little.

Once you have calculated takt time and pitch; determined minimum buffer and safety stocks; performed labor and machine balancing; and stabilized WIP, you are ready to proceed to the next phase. Review the WIP checklist (Figure 2-18), which provides structure for your WIP activities. (This checklist will later be used in conjunction with Figure 4-6 in relation to methods of tracking production.) If you have completed numbers 1 through 9 on this checklist, you are ready to standardize the system. (Number 10 on the WIP checklist will be discussed in the next chapter in the section on creating an address system.)

You already understand the importance of stability in your operations. Reviewing the labor and process capability in relation to demand allows you to determine staffing

---

**WIP Checklist**

1. What is the footprint for required space?

    a. What is the size of the WIP in square feet?

    b. What is the amount of WIP in days or hours on hand for each tool or product?

2. Is WIP located according to supplier process or customer process?

3. Does the bin size match the final pack-out quantity or is pack-out divisible by pieces/bin?

4. Are minimum and maximum levels established?

5. Have bin height limits been established?

6. If yes, are RED and YELLOW signals established?

    ❑ When your WIP level reaches the RED line, it means to STOP producing—maximum amount is in place.

    ❑ When your WIP level reaches the YELLOW line, it is a warning; need to PRODUCE this product or color—minimum has been reached.

7. Is FIFO (first in, first out) established?

8. Is there visual control?

9. Is there a part or picture hanging above each row for easy identification of what is being produced there?

10. Do you have WIP address location cards in place and color-coded to press?

---

**Figure 2-18.** WIP Checklist

and equipment requirements. The next section of this book addresses process standardization through visual tools. These tools, described in the next two chapters, will help you determine if you are producing to takt and where you may need to take corrective action.

# Stage II. Standardize

Production layout must support flow, and production processes and methods must be standardized. Flow ensures that the value stream receives the right parts at the right time in the correct amounts. It also ensures that a value stream never produces more than a customer requires. The ideal goal of flow production is "one-piece flow" or "move one, make one." This is production to takt time.

Production cells and supermarkets assist flow in a visual pull system. You can see the flow, and you can see where flow has stopped. Quick changeover methods and autonomous maintenance need to be in place for your cells to function smoothly and meet takt time/pitch standards.

Once the layout of cells and supermarkets establishes the possibility of achieving one-piece flow, you must develop a visual communication system throughout the production process. The next two chapters lead you through the creation of a visual system in layout, address, and production processes that you will need to standardize the production flow. The entire production system should visually communicate at every step what is *supposed* to go on and what *is* going on. This visual system of structures and process tools is the heart of lean manufacturing.

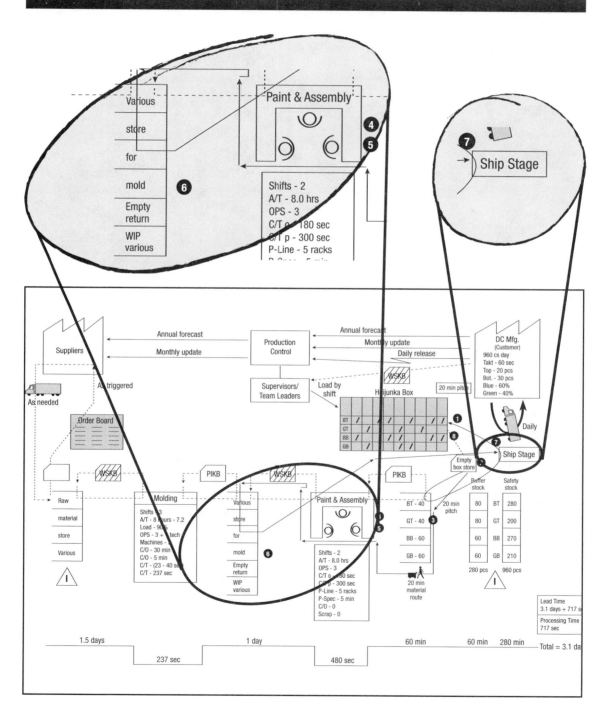

# Chapter 3. Visual Layout and Visual Address System

The visual structures of pull production include the layout—production cells, a supermarket system, and the ship stage—as well as an address system for the plant. Both are discussed in this chapter. A visual communication system also includes production tally boards, unit count boards, and the raw material order board, discussed in Chapter 4, Visual Production Process. The heijunka box is also part of this visual structure and will be discussed in detail in Chapter 5. The heijunka box is the culmination of your pull system; when installed, it facilitates simplifying the entire production control process. But first, you must establish the visual layout and communication processes discussed in this chapter.

## Production Cells

Many of you have heard of U-shaped cells, but it is wise to remember that there are many letters in the alphabet. Use common sense in designing your cells to establish the labor balance and flow. SLMS used the U-shape design. Other companies have used H, Y, F, or parallel designs to achieve more or less the same purpose. The take home message here is that a generic term should not dictate your cell design.

Visualize the process. Use the paper doll method: Draw processes to scale and cut them out. Call the team together to move the pieces around until you come up with an acceptable design to test. This allows you the freedom to work through the potential variations before going to the shop floor. Once a design has been selected, make sure you review it with the necessary support organizations (maintenance, engineering, etc.) to get their buy in.

All the data you gathered and the calculations you made in your self-evaluation (described in the previous chapter) are based on your layout. Designing production cells shifts the plant layout from a focus on process islands to a focus on value stream.

At SLMS, the molding, paint, and assembly operations were separate functions in the current state map. A robotic painting operation painted the arms in big batches. In the future state, thanks to an employee's redesign idea, a smaller paint/drying tool allowed SLMS to combine paint and assembly into one production cell.

An evaluation of the molding operation, on the other hand, determined that SLMS had to run three shifts of the molding machine because of the capital costs the equipment represented. SLMS installed an in-process supermarket from which paint/assembly now withdraws material at regular intervals based on pitch.

A kaizen event reduced tool change times. This cut the time to such an extent SLMS began running every tool every day instead of running molding in large batches. Eventually, SLMS was able to run every tool multiple times a day. In this case, WIP was reduced to less than a day in the supermarket at any time. SLMS now had stability and flow from the customer back through the molding process.

---

### Monuments to Overproduction

Large, centralized or shared machines called "monuments" often interrupt flow. These immovable machines are designed to produce in batches. They are usually capital-intensive, have long setup times, and are difficult, if not impossible, to move into the value stream. To eliminate the interruptions to flow—or at the very least minimize them—plan to use right-sized equipment for future products. Right-sized equipment fits into a value stream and allows all operations to be included in a cell and done in one-piece flow. Right-sized equipment is usually small, simple, and easy to move. It is designed to be financially practical so that it can be dedicated to a single cell.

---

Until you can move to a condition where all your equipment is right-sized, or if you have equipment that cannot be right-sized, you can do what SLMS did—create a process that feeds the assembly cell through an in-process supermarket and manage the output of that process through production instruction kanbans initiated by triggers from the supermarket. (Production instruction kanbans are discussed further in Chapter 4.) A supermarket is a location for storage of a set amount of finished goods or WIP within the value stream that allow for a pull system when pure continuous flow is not possible. Reduction of setup times is critical if you are to make this sort of change with the monuments in your process.

## In-Process and Finished Goods Supermarkets

In the example of the SLMS molding operation in the previous chapter, an in-process supermarket was established at the molding function. Wherever obstacles to continuous flow exist, you can use in-process supermarkets to maintain the takt image of production. An in-process supermarket system is particularly useful wherever you have multiple demands on a machine or a process, where more than one value stream is served by a single operation and where there is a high degree of commonality among parts. As you improve flow, right-size your equipment, and reduce WIP, the need for in-process supermarkets may decrease. The ideal state is one-piece flow to takt time. Supermarkets are compromises, albeit necessary ones, to this ideal. So are pitch and buffer and safety inventories.

You may choose to create a finished goods supermarket and use FIFO (first in, first out) to deliver product that the customer has pulled from your operation. The preferred method, the one that SLMS chose, is to pull directly from assembly to a ship stage area. SLMS accomplished this by creating a two-container system of finished goods and raw material at its assembly line. This two-container system allows the material handler to complete his or her route, picking up finished goods and replenishing raw materials, ensuring that the customer for the raw material—assembly—will not run out of stock. The quantity in the raw material containers should match, in most cases, the pitch quantity. Once again, please use common sense. For example, if you have small screws (or like product), it may be more practical to have a larger quantity or bulk quantity on the line. Remember that the smallest container on the line will use less space, thereby reducing the walk time of the assembly operators, so please use caution when making this decision (see Figure 3-1).

| **SLMS Finished Goods** | | | | |
|---|---|---|---|---|
| **Before** | | **After—line side** **two container system** | | |
| | *Warehouse* | *Line side* | *Buffer stock* | *Safety stock* |
| Blue Tops | 3000 | 40 | 80 | 280 |
| Green Tops | 3000 | 40 | 80 | 200 |
| Blue Bottoms | 4200 | 60 | 60 | 270 |
| Green Bottoms | 2100 | 60 | 60 | 210 |

**Figure 3-1.** SLMS Two-container System

## Ship Stage and Staging Lanes for Finished Product

It is now time to organize the shipping area. With the help of your buffer and safety stocks, you can be shipping to customer order while you continue to establish the rest of your pull system upstream.

Establishing staging lanes near the dock where the delivery truck or train picks up shipments stabilizes and standardizes the value stream's shipping process by visually communicating to the material route person how much product goes into each lane. A ship stage tally sheet (Figures 3-4 and 3-5) allows a visual check, assuring that you ship exactly what the customer has ordered and when the order is needed. Organizing shipping for continuous service has three basic tasks:

1. Establish the ship stage area.
2. Determine shipping restrictions.
3. Create and use a ship tally sheet

## Establish the Ship Stage Area

You must determine a specific place in your facility that will be used for your ship stage area. This area is used for staging the next shipment or shipments that will be sent to customers.

Mark off how much space you will need for staging lanes (sometimes called shipping areas or shipping lanes). Depending on what occurs in your plant, you will designate staging areas for each customer, destination, or shipping time. For example, if you supply several plants for the same customer, you will have to designate staging areas for each destination. If you make multiple shipments daily to a single customer destination, establish staging areas by time. See Figure 3-2 for an example of a ship stage area.

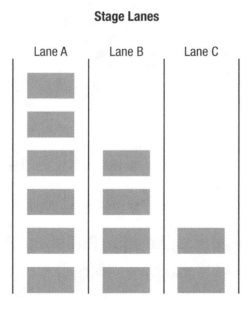

**Figure 3-2.** Ship Stage Area

Establish your ship stage area using the following guidelines:

- Completely empty out the designated area.
- Clean it thoroughly.
- Draw a map that defines the area required.
- Return only what is needed to the area, based on the map.
- Establish shipping lanes or areas by putting in place visual indicators.

### Determine Shipping Restrictions

Ask yourself the following questions to determine whether the customer imposes any specific shipping instructions:

1. Are there any pack height restrictions?
2. Can you mix products on a skid?
3. Can you ship partial skids?
4. Can you spot a trailer when volume warrants?
5. What are the minimum or maximum weight restrictions?

Review and use the Ship Stage Checklist (see Figure 3-3) as you set up your ship stage area and post requirements on the reverse side of the ship stage tally sheet.

**Ship Stage Checklist**

1. How have the shipping lanes been established?
   By customer?
   By destination?
   By time of delivery?
   For empty returnable containers and skids?
2. Are the buffer and safety stock rotation plans posted and being followed?
3. Are the buffer and safety stock withdrawal logs posted and being used correctly?
4. What are the shipping restrictions, if any?
   Are there any pack height restrictions?
   Can you mix product on a skid?
   Can you ship partial skids?
   Can you spot a trailer when volume warrants?
   Will you use returnable or disposable shipping containers?
   What are finish pack requirements?
   What are the minimum or maximum weight restrictions?

**Figure 3-3.** Ship Stage Checklist

## Create and use a ship stage tally sheet

You should use a ship stage tally to confirm that the staged quantities conform to the customer's requirements. Figure 3-4 shows a recommended format and the minimum required information to be put on the ship stage tally.

A ship stage tally should be located at each ship stage lane, placed on a clipboard that will be hung on a short post. The instructions for filling out the tally sheet should be posted on the back of the clipboard. There should be one tally for each shipment. If you ship three times per day to the same customer, the process might involve three distinct ship stage areas, and you need a separate ship stage tally for each shipment.

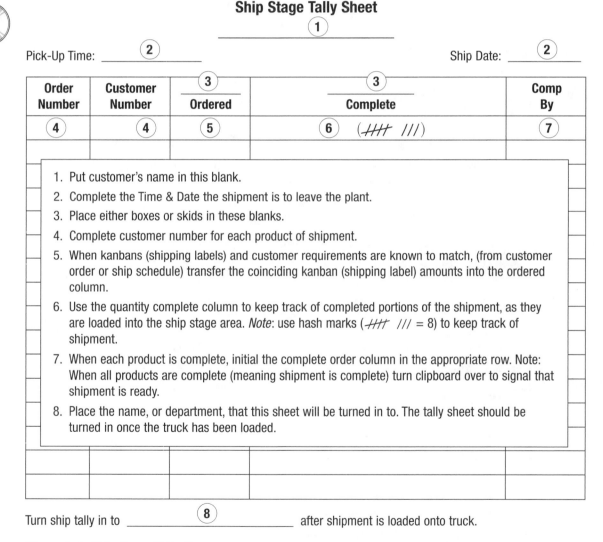

Figure 3-4. Ship Stage Tally Sheet

SLMS, for example, ships three times daily to DC Mfg, Inc. It established three staging lanes in shipping and a separate ship stage tally for each shipment. SLMS set up a simple tally sheet stand—the implementation team got a used plastic bucket, put a wooden post through it, filled it with cement, and hung the tally sheet from the post!

As they delivered to the ship stage lanes, material handlers marked the tally sheet (see Figure 3-5). The SLMS implementation team discovered it was best to use strokes and hash marks, not numbers, to record each skid delivered to the staging area. A numerical system was tried for a while, but people made mistakes adding the numbers. They made virtually no mistakes by putting a hash mark through every four strokes to indicate five deliveries had been made.

### Ship Stage Tally Sheet
#### Garden Lane

Pick-Up Time:  4:00 PM                                                    Ship Date:  6/7

| Internal Number | Customer Number | Ordered | Complete | Comp By |
|---|---|---|---|---|
| 5678 | SA98-001T | 29 | ╫╫ ╫╫ /// | |
| | | | | |
| 6789 | S98-002T | 13 | ╫╫ // | |
| | | | | |
| 1234 | S98-003B | 29 | ╫╫ ╫╫ /// | |
| | | | | |
| 2345 | S-98-004B | 13 | ╫╫ // | |
| | | | | |
| | | | | |
| | | | | |
| | | | | |
| | | | | |
| | | | | |
| | | | | |
| | | | | |
| | | | | |

Turn ship tally in to D. T. after shipment is loaded onto truck.

**Figure 3-5.** SLMS Ship Stage Tally Sheet—Filled In

Today, when an order is complete, the supervisor initials the ship stage tally sheet and turns it over. The back of the sheet already reads: SHIPMENT READY. The ship stage tally allows the material handler to place the container in the proper ship lane. If lane A, ship time 4:00 P.M., has the required amount of product for green tops, the material handlers automatically know that they must place the next container of green tops in lane B.

## Visual Address System

Imagine driving into an unfamiliar town and trying to find a house, where there are no street signs, and worse, no addresses. How can you find your way around? The same principle applies to factories and even offices. Without addresses and signboards of some kind, only the most experienced employees know where to find things. Everyone else is at a loss.

An address system is a road map that tells people precisely where they are, where material is located, and where it needs to be taken. For a pull system to run smoothly, the exact locations where parts and materials are stored must have "addresses" so that material handlers can locate and deliver the right items to the right places. The address system will help you standardize well-ordered routes for the material handlers to follow. An address system helps keep the plant in order at all times, and, in this respect, is a logical extension of your 5S activities. From a safety standpoint, too, you need an address system to direct emergency personnel in the event of an accident or a fire. "Go to area C4" is more precise than "Go to press 2." A good grid system also makes training easier. To turn a factory into a visual workplace where you can see where everything belongs—at a glance—you need a good facility address system. A facility address system operates on the same principles as any address system would—from the general to the specific. With the focus on inventory management, use the following prompts to create a workable address system:

- Where are you in the plant?
- Which direction are you facing?
- Which row, rack, or conveyor is something on?
- Which shelf is something on?
- Where on a shelf is something located?

If you have an existing address system that is easy to understand and is a good visual tool for managing the plant, continue to use it. You can adapt and simplify the addressing strategy described in this section to suit your own operations. Any address system will do, but you must have one. The basis of an address system is a grid pattern of numbers and letters.

## Step 1

Use the plant's support columns to divide the plant into a grid and label the columns with numbers and letters. Pick one of the four corners of the building as a point of origin (0,0).Begin from the point of origin and label one row of columns with letters (A, B, C, D, E, etc.). Label the columns running at a right angle from the point of origin with numbers (1, 2, 3, 4, 5, 6, etc.). All locations will then have a letter and a number designation (E5, D3, etc.). See Figure 3-6 for an example an address system grid.

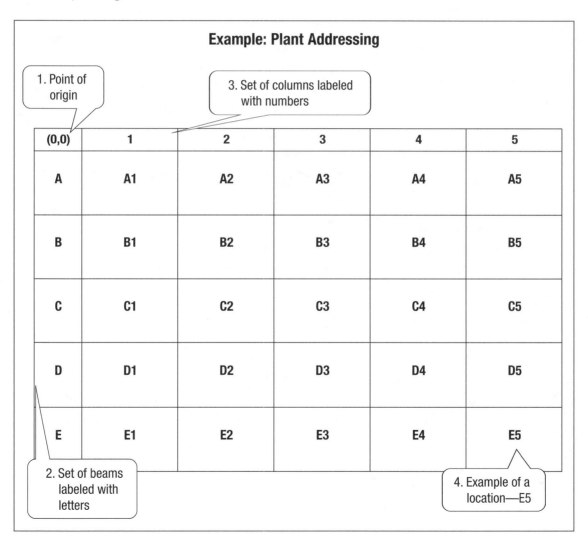

**Example: Plant Addressing**

| 1. Point of origin | | 3. Set of columns labeled with numbers | | | |
|---|---|---|---|---|---|
| **(0,0)** | **1** | **2** | **3** | **4** | **5** |
| **A** | **A1** | **A2** | **A3** | **A4** | **A5** |
| **B** | **B1** | **B2** | **B3** | **B4** | **B5** |
| **C** | **C1** | **C2** | **C3** | **C4** | **C5** |
| **D** | **D1** | **D2** | **D3** | **D4** | **D5** |
| **E** | **E1** | **E2** | **E3** | **E4** | **E5** |

2. Set of beams labeled with letters

4. Example of a location—E5

**Figure 3-6.** Plant Address Grid

## Step 2

Next create a complete address to identify the rows and racks where materials are stored, either in a supermarket or at the point of use at a production line or cell. For your material handlers or anyone else to locate parts, you will need more precise addresses than the two-position address denoting the grid quadrant. The plant address may have a minimum of six positions:

$$1\,2 - 3\,4\,5\,6$$

Not every part number will need six positions, but this system, while easy to understand, gives you flexibility if you do need all six positions. This six-position address will appear on the kanban system explained in Chapter 4.

Each position from 1 to 6 takes you from the most general to the most specific location in the plant. As shown in the example in Figure 3-7, positions #1 and #2 give the address location of the bay where the product can be found. Facing in the direction of #3, and starting in the left position of the bay (#1 and #2), number the rows from left to right (1, 2, 3, etc.). Figure 3-7 shows a general grid.

---

**SLMS Molding, Inc.**

**General Address**

1     2     —     3     4     5     —     6

1 = Letter of main grid address (i.e. A, B, C, etc.).

2 = Number of main grid address (i.e. 1, 2, 3, etc.).
    Together #1 and #2 give the address location of the bay where the product can be found.

3 = Refers to the direction you are facing (N, S, E, W), either at point of use or point of store.

4 = Refers to a particular row, rack, or conveyor where the particular product is located.
    Facing in direction in #3, starting in the left position of the bay (#1 and #2), number the rows from **left to right** (1, 2, 3, etc.).

5 = This is used in special cases only. Most of the time this position will be left blank. This location is used when there is more than one rack or row deep of product in one bay, (looking in the same direction).

6 = Refers to shelf location within a particular row or rack (1, 2, 3, etc.). Number shelves from **bottom to top**.

---

**Figure 3-7.** Example of a Plant Address

## Step 3

Create signboards that are easy to see and read and that won't get covered up. It does little good to have an address system that is difficult to understand or hidden behind something. Your signboards are the method by which you communicate the system to everyone who enters the plant. In fact, you should consider your audience to be someone who is not a regular worker in the plant. This approach will help you create an address system that will allow anyone to find anything in the plant easily and quickly. You will need signboards that hang from the ceiling and/or high on the walls displaying main grid addresses, as well as signs on racks showing inventory type and quantity. Signs displaying the main grid address should be approximately 3 feet by 2 feet and hung in the center of each quadrant of the grid. Use this same system to create standard addresses for assembly, WIP, and raw materials. A set of common rules (along with a few exceptions to these) follows:

*Assembly address*

1. Use the letters N, S, E, and W to refer to the direction you must face to find the correct location for the material. If the material handler is delivering parts to assembly and must face west to find and fill that particular rack, then the #3 position of the address would be a W.

2. Number each assembly rack from left to right (1, 2, 3, etc.) This is represented in position #4 of the address.

3. Number each shelf on each rack, also, starting from the bottom shelf and going to the top (1, 2, 3, etc.). This corresponds to position #6 of the address.

In the example in Figure 3-8, address A2-W4-2C indicates that the material handler brings raw material for assembly to bay A2 and faces west in the bay. He finds the fourth rack, counting from the left of the bay, finds the second shelf up from the

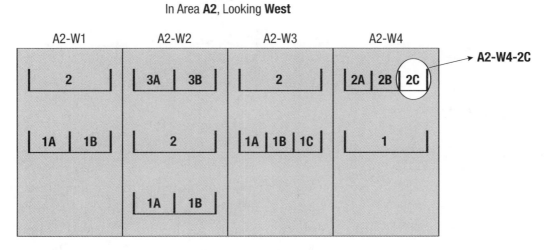

**Figure 3-8.** Example of Assembly Address System

bottom and places a container into slot C. If proper signboards have been made, the location of racks and containers should be easily identified without the handler having to count.

## WIP address

1. The direction (N, S, E, W) always refers to the direction you are facing. In other words, if you face South to remove product from WIP, then position #3 of the address would be S.

2. Number each WIP store from left to right (i.e., 1, 2, 3, etc.) and put this in position #4 of the WIP address.

3. If there are multiple shelves in a WIP store, number each shelf from bottom to top. This is represented in position #6 of the WIP address.

In the example in Figure 3-9, address B2-W5-2, the material handler takes the kanban card to bay B2 and faces west in the bay. He finds the fifth rack, counting from the left of the bay, and removes a container from the second shelf up from the bottom of rack 5 and places the kanban into the container.

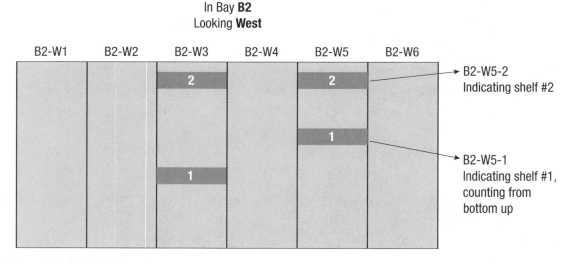

**Figure 3-9.** WIP Address System

## WIP address card

The WIP Card, which displays a visual address, is mounted at the storage point in the WIP area. In a FIFO (first-in, first-out) system, there is a fill side and a pull side to the address card. This card serves both purposes (see Figure 3-10). WIP is normally addressed on the pull side only, using the standard form. If the WIP is located

**Pull Side**

WIP Address ID Card

Plant Address:

N3-W1

Part #:

98-014

Description:

Bottom Cap

Color:

Blue

WIPADD.WDB

**Fill Side**

WIP Address ID Card

Press #:

1

Tool #:

S98-014

| High | Deep | Total | Bin Qty |
|------|------|-------|---------|
| 4 | 3 | 20 | 30 |

Container: **A**

Description:

Bottom Cap

| Part #: | Color: |
|---------|--------|
| | Blue |

WIPADD.WDB

**Figure 3-10.** WIP Address Card

close to the producing process, you may not need an address on the fill side. If the WIP is stored away from the producing process, you may need a delivery address on the fill side.

The fill side gives the producing side the information needed to replenish the parts from that tool or process. The pull side gives an address and description to help the material handlers identify the location or area in the supermarket where they obtain product to replenish the assembly line. The route of the material handler is discussed in Chapter 5.

You must have one WIP address card for each product or color that the individual processes produce. This card is placed in the WIP supermarket area and is used in conjunction with the production instruction kanban for that tool or process and with the parts withdrawal/supply kanban. The kanban system is described in detail in Chapter 4.

## Raw Material Racks

It is recommended that a material rack be no longer than 8 to 10 feet from upright to upright. One address would be the area from upright to upright, which in most cases would be about 8 feet. (See Figure 3-11 for an example.) For addressing purposes,

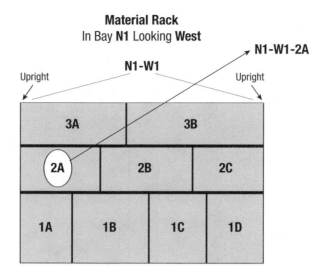

**Figure 3-11.** Example of Material Rack Address System

give one address to a material rack, as defined above. When addressing material racks, follow the same rules illustrated in Figure 3-9.

Once you understand that a visual system must be in place in the layout of your value stream, you are ready to move into the visual production part of the process. In Chapter 4, the discussion turns to the tools that you will use to standardize and to assist operators, including the material handler, in performing their tasks. The chapter also examines how each part of this process is connected to each element of the value stream.

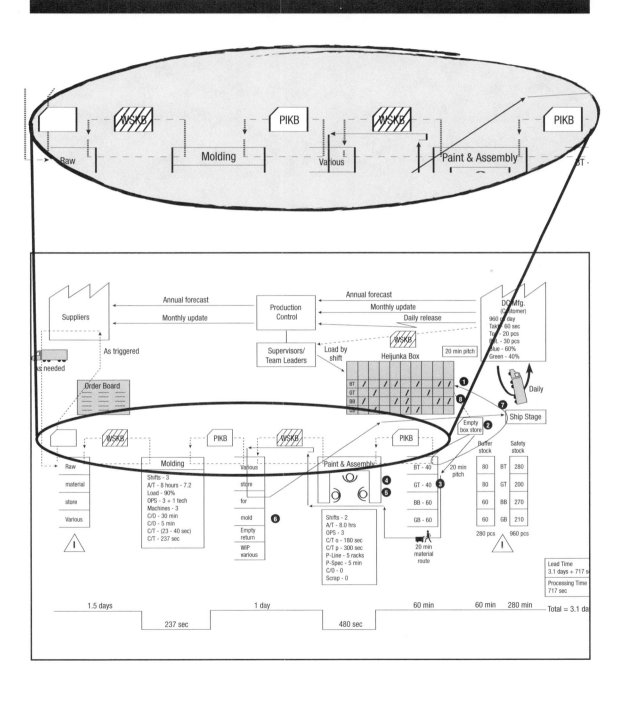

# Chapter 4. Visual Production Process

## Standardized Work

Standardized work is perhaps the most difficult element of your lean system to implement. People are not machines. They want to do things their own way, and they like to vary the way they do things from time to time. For this reason, implementing standardized work and keeping it implemented requires constant vigilance.

Toyota plants often reinforce standardized work by having a team leader for every six to eight people on the line. The team leader constantly monitors how the operators are doing their work, comparing the process to the standardized worksheets that specify how the work is to be done.

Supervisors and operators understand that standardized work is not a limitation or an inspection of operators. In fact, they recognize that if everyone does tasks the same way, a baseline from which to improve is established. Moreover, they realize that standardized work, which is paced and balanced to takt time, reveals abnormalities and improvement opportunities.

### Benefits of Standardized Work

Truly lean companies know that standardized work can keep them a step ahead of the competition. The many benefits of standardized processes make the discipline well worth your commitment. One of the most important of these benefits is that operators appreciate having the standards set for their operations because standards facilitate a total grasp of what needs to be done and how. To summarize, standardized work allows operators:

- To know the best sequences and times for each operation
- To perform to these standards continuously, knowing they are doing the work correctly
- To move where they are needed when they are needed and continue performing to established standards to balance labor in relation to customer demand

In addition, standardized work provides an ideal framework for:

- Setting baselines for improvements
- Simplifying training of new people on the line
- Sustaining consistent productivity, quality, and safety

## Guidelines for Standardized Work

Standardized work ensures that everyone who performs assembly operations will do so correctly and with the right tools, materials, and inventory precisely where and when needed. For consistent and level flow to occur within the manufacturing value stream, and within each cell that you create, you need to know that whoever is doing the work will be producing to the same takt time and achieving a consistent cycle time for the work elements assigned. There are a few guidelines to observe when you implement standardized work:

1. Work with operators to determine the most efficient work methods.
2. Get consensus among the operators to encourage buy-in.
3. Do not compromise takt time—adhere to it.
4. Use *operator instruction sheets* to train staff, and give managers written standards that they can use as they supervise work.
5. Be flexible. As takt time and/or cycle time changes, so will resource allocation.

## Operator Instruction Sheets

A standard operator instruction sheet lists the standard sequence in which the work should be done. There are a number of reasons for creating a standard operator instruction sheet:

1. It gives the plant an accurate set of instructions to train the staff in the operation of the facility.
2. It gives the staff members a list of instructions to follow as they complete their tasks.
3. It allows management to confirm that the staff is following the standard.
4. It develops a standard that will safely produce a quality product in the most efficient way within the allocated takt time.

To create operator instruction sheets (see example in Figure 4-1b), use white paper, 11 × 17 or larger, for easy visibility. Put each operation or assembly point on a separate sheet of paper and hang each sheet near its corresponding workstation. Consistent color-coding of the steps in the process will help operators clearly distinguish

## Operator Instruction Sheet

| | | |
|---|---|---|
| 1. | Customer | Name of the customer |
| 2. | Part # | Part number |
| 3. | Part Name | Name of the part |
| 4. | Operation | The operation this sheet refers to. It may include any of: |

|  | | |
|---|---|---|
| From: | WIP Box | To: F/G Box |
| From: | 1 | To: 15 |
| From: | PFC Seq. #1 | To: PFC Seq. #8 |

| | | |
|---|---|---|
| 5. | Department | The department this sheet is used in |
| 6. | Group | The group within the department |
| 7. | Dept. Mgr. Approval | Department manager approval |
| 8. | Quality Approval | Quality manager or engineer approval |
| 9. | Engineering Approval | Manufacturing engineering approval |
| 10. | Print Level | The latest print level that this part is being produced to |
| 11. | Revision Date | The date that this sheet was revised |
| 12. | GM Approval | General manager approval |
| 13. | Elmnt. # | The sequential job element number—1, 2, 3, etc. |
| 14. | Work Element | A description of the element. The work element needs to be as brief and as clear as possible. Use the "Key Point" section to elaborate or clarify the work element. |
| 15. | Elmnt. Time | The time it takes to perform that element |
| 16. | K | The Key Point number that relates to the element—i.e., if element is #4, then Key Point would be #4. |
| 17. | Key Points | A description of the Key Points. For example: |

|  | |
|---|---|
| Work Element would be: | Activate fixture |
| Key Point would be: | Close lid to activate |

| | | |
|---|---|---|
| 18. | SYMB | Place the standard symbol from 20 here |
| 19. | Diagram of Work Seq. | This area is reserved for the Work Sequence. The Work Sequence is the most critical information in this area. Additional information such as sequence of steps, part sketches, and pictures may be included as appropriate. |
| 20. | Symbols | The symbols that could be placed in item 17 |

*Note:* One additional symbol is permitted:

**E = Ease** of operation may be added

| | | |
|---|---|---|
| 21. | Page ___ of ___ | The page number of the document |

*Note:* The location for the Document # is in the upper right hand corner of the sheet (located above print level). In addition, a File name may be added to the bottom left hand corner of the sheet.

**Figure 4-1a.** Directions for Completing Operator Instruction Sheet

## Operator Instruction Sheet

| Customer: | ① | Operation: | ④ | Dept. Mgr. Approval: | ⑦ | Print Level: | ⑩ |
| Part #: | ② | Department: | ⑤ | Quality Approval: | ⑧ | Revision Date: | ⑪ |
| Part Name: | ③ | Group: | ⑥ | Engineering Approval: | ⑨ | GM Approval: | ⑫ |

| Elmnt. # | Work Element | Elmnt. Time | K | Key Points | Sym | Diagram of Work Sequence, (may include pack instructions, pictures) |
|---|---|---|---|---|---|---|
| ⑬ | ⑭ | ⑮ | ⑯ | ⑰ | ⑱ | ⑲ |
| | | | | | | |
| | | | | | | |
| | | | | | | |
| | | | | | | |
| | | | | | | |

▽ Critical Defect ● Standard In-Process Stock ◇ Quality Check ✚ Safety ⑳

Page ㉑ of ____

㉑

Figure 4-1b. Operator Instruction Sheet

which steps of the job are to be performed at each station in the process. The following sequence of colors is one possibility:

| STEP | HIGHLIGHT COLOR |
|---|---|
| First station in the process | Blue |
| Second station in the process | Yellow |
| Third station in the process | Green |
| Fourth station in the process | Orange |

If you have more than four stations, additional colors can be left to the discretion of the division manager. Note, however, that the selected color sequence must be the same for all operator instruction sheets in the plant. Using this method, anyone looking at a sheet in any department can easily tell where a job starts.

In filling out the operator instruction sheet, have your quality organization assist in identifying the key points for operators to follow. This is important because it is these key points in the operation or process that have the greatest potential for quality problems.

### How to Create the Operator Instruction Sheet and Use It for Training

1. Figures 2-2a and 2-2b in Chapter 2 (Cycle Time Worksheet Instructions and Operator Cycle Time Worksheet respectively) can be used as the foundation for the Standardized Work on the Operator Instruction Sheet.

2. Write the job instructions *with an operator* by your side, in the sequence in which the individual tasks of the operation or process are to be performed. It is critical that you include the operators in this step as they are the ones who will be doing the work and will most likely know the best methods.

   **Note:** Instructions must be written clearly, but as briefly as possible.

3. Train the operator(s) how to do the job as follows:

   | YOU | | STUDENT/OPERATOR | |
   |---|---|---|---|
   | Tell | Do | Listen | Watch |
   | Tell | Watch | Listen | Do |
   | Tell | Do | Listen | Watch |
   | Tell | Watch | Listen | Do |
   | Listen | Watch | Tell | Do |

   Once this sequence is complete and the student/operator feels comfortable and has had time to perform the job a number of times, the job is videotaped. The time allowed depends on the complexity of the job.

4. Tape the job again. Review the tape with the operator, or operators if more than one shift is involved. Compare the actions performed to the operator instruction sheet and use operator input to improve the job.

Figure 4-2 shows an example of an operator instruction sheet completed at SLMS. Note that the completed document lists specific work elements of key points as well as a diagram with a visible representation of the work sequence. Words and pictures reinforce each other and make the instruction sheet especially useful.

## Color-Coded Kanban System

The kanban system—often called the nervous system of pull production, and sometimes incorrectly called pull production itself—is a critical component of the visual production process and of standardization. It is with the initiation of a kanban system that pull production goes into action.

Kanban in Japanese simply means "card" or "sign" and refers to the inventory control cards used in a pull system. Kanbans are the written instructions to withdraw material or produce product. The circulation of kanbans links customer orders to production orders, moving upstream through the assembly and production processes all the way to raw material orders. The kanban system follows some important rules that distinguish pull production from push production:

1. Downstream operations or cells withdraw items from upstream operations or cells.

2. Upstream operations or cells produce only when withdrawal kanbans from downstream operations remove enough material from the WIP supermarket to trigger a production-instruction kanban for their operation or process.

3. An operation produces only the amount indicated on each production-instruction kanban.

4. Each operation sends only 100 percent defect-free products downstream.

SLMS put in place a two-container system, which ensured that the assembly operation would not run out of parts. There was a slight variation in the material handler's ability to get back to the exact delivery spot in every pitch loop, so a second container was put in place to ensure flow. As you create your own kanban system, you will need to take similar variations into account.

## SLMS Molding, Inc.
## Operator Instruction Sheet

| Customer: Garden Lane | Operation: Strut Assembly | Dept. Mgr. Approval: | Print Level: C6-30 |
|---|---|---|---|
| Part #: xxxx | Department: Strut | Quality Approval: | Revision Date: 4/03 |
| Part Name: Top and Bottom Strut | Group: | Engineering Approval: | GM Approval: |

Diagram of Work Sequence, (may include pack instructions, pictures)

| Elmnt. # | Work Element | Elmnt. Time | K | Key Points | Sym |
|---|---|---|---|---|---|
| 1 | Paint Bottom and Top Cap and pass to left and right | 12 | | | |
| 2 | Add Top Clip | 10 | | | |
| 3 | Inspect Top | 4 | | Check paint and ensure secure fit of cap | |
| 4 | Pack Top | 8 | | When a container is complete, move to finish slide and select new container. Look at production instruction and go to step one. | |
| 5 | Add Bottom Clip | 14 | | | |
| 6 | Inspect Bottom | 4 | | Check paint and ensure secure fit of cap | |
| 7 | Pack Bottom | 8 | | When a container is complete, move to finish slide and select new container. Look at production instruction and go to step one. | |
| | | | | | |
| | | | | | |
| | | | | | |
| | | | | | |

▽ Critical Defect     ● Standard In-Process Stock     ◇ Quality Check     ✚ Safety

Figure 4-2. Operator Instruction Sheet at SLMS

To create your kanban system, start by color coding your production processes, then create the kanbans as described below. There are three primary types of kanbans you will use—parts-withdrawal kanbans, withdrawal/supply kanbans, and production-instruction kanbans. Parts-withdrawal kanbans are normally customer orders. In the section below, we discuss withdrawal/supply kanbans (WSKB) and production-instruction kanbans (PIKB).

## Workstation Color-Coding System

Color coding all the processes, machines, and stores and using these color codes on the kanbans greatly enhances the efficiency of your pull production system. The simpler and more visual you make your process, the easier it will be for everyone to learn the system and the smoother it will run.

Designate a color for each machine or processing center. For instance, if there are eight machines or processes, then you will have eight different colors, one for each machine or process (e.g., machine 1 = blue, machine 2 = green, etc.).

All WIP produced on the same machine or process will be color coded to match the specific press or process. If products A, B, and C are run on machine 1, which is blue, then the addresses for products A, B, and C will be blue. If a tool or part runs on more than one machine, color code the WIP to match the primary machine it runs on. The color of the WIP address card (see Figure 3-11), on both the Fill and the Pull sides will match the color of the associated press.

The production-instruction kanban will also be color coded to match the respective machine or process. Thus the production-instruction kanbans for products A, B, and C in our example will be blue: In other words, the product runs on the blue machine and is stored in the blue WIP location.

Break the assembly area into smaller operational areas and assign colors to each area. An assembly area with several operations can be broken down by workstation, and each workstation is assigned its own color (workstation 1=blue, workstation 2=green, etc.). The main objective is to break the assembly area into smaller color-coded sections, creating a visual aid for the material handler who will be delivering materials and retrieving parts to and from the various stations in the assembly cell.

The color of the kanbans will be the same color as the appropriate color-coded WIP store (the storage point). The colored dot on the kanbans will be the same as the color-coded section in the assembly area (the use point). Thus, a blue kanban means the product can be found in the blue WIP storage area and is produced at the blue machine process. A green dot means the product needs to be delivered to the point of use, which is located in the green area in assembly or the next customer in the process.

At SLMS, originally, all the kanbans were white, but this caused confusion and delays. Material handlers used carts to pick up empty containers and withdrawal kanbans from assembly, then went "shopping" for raw materials at a central storage area, withdrawing full containers from racks, placing them on their carts, and bringing them back to various locations at the assembly cell. Because the kanbans were the same color, handlers had to sort them by area, a time-consuming process. By color coding the workstations and matching kanbans, SLMS made it easier and faster for material handlers to sort the kanbans according to the storage location of the replenishment material.

Keep in mind that the supply area may serve different colored delivery areas. In the kanban card example in Figure 4-3, the material sorted in the blue area is used in the white area, as indicated by the gold square (represented by the shaded square) in the upper right corner of the kanban. This allows the handlers to arrange the raw material efficiently on their carts for the return delivery trip to assembly. They can set up the new boxes so that all the material going to the gold area is kept together, separated from material going to the green area, and so on.

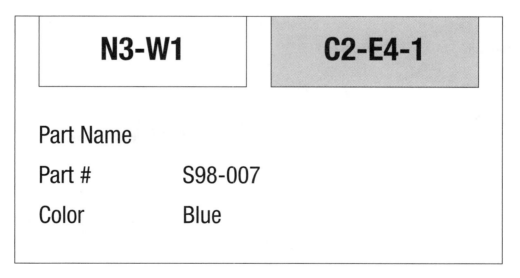

**Figure 4-3.** Kanban with Color Coding

Once at the supermarket, material handlers walk a prescribed route through the color-coded areas. In the green area, they pull all the green kanbans from the pockets on their carts, look at the storage address on the kanban, walk to that location, and pull a filled container. They repeat the process in each color-coded area.

## Parts Withdrawal/Supply Kanbans

**SLMS Molding, Inc.**

**Parts Withdrawal/Supply Kanban**

Standard Kanban

| Store Address | Use Address |
|---|---|
| (1) | (2) |

(6)

Part Name: _____ (3) _____

Part #: _____ (4) _____

Color: _____ (5) _____

The recommendation is to put the following information on both sides of the Kanban.

| 1. Store Address | Storage location of product |
|---|---|
| 2. Use Address | Use location of product |
| 3. Part Name | Name of part |
| 4. Part # | Part number |
| 5. Color | Color of part if necessary |
| 6. Color Dot | Color dot (3/4″) will be same color as use point color (i.e., if the point of use location is color coded **blue**, then the dot would be **blue**). |

**Figure 4-4.** Parts Withdrawal/Supply Kanban

Parts withdrawal/supply kanbans (see Figure 4-4) are used by one process to "pull" parts from the upstream process. The material handler must know where to go to get the various products that the customers are requesting. The address systems that you create will play an important role in this process. Addresses will be put on the parts withdrawal/supply kanbans and color coded to identify specific areas where parts are stored and where they are used. This is how the system works:

A.  The operator removes a kanban from the supply container.

B.  The operator places the kanban within reach of the material handler on a kanban post.

C. The material handler picks up the kanban on his or her route.

D. The material handler places the kanban in the matching colored holder on the material cart (i.e., if it is a yellow kanban, it is placed in the yellow holder on the cart).

E. The material handler goes to the storage area and pulls from the holder kanbans that match the color-coded store (i.e., if at yellow storage area, he pulls all yellow kanbans from the holder).

F. The handler then looks at the storage address on the kanban and locates the correct container (i.e., if the address is N3-W1, the handler goes to that location).

G. The handler places the kanban in the container and puts the container, with the kanban, on the cart.

H. The handler goes to the use point (assembly area) and pulls from the cart the containers that match the color-coded use point. The colored block or dot on the kanban will match the color code of the use point (i.e., if the handler is at the purple use point, the colored dot on the kanban should be purple).

I. The handler looks at the use point address on the kanban to locate the delivery point (i.e., if the use point address is C2-E4-1, he or she goes to that location).

J. The handler delivers the container to that location.

   **Note:** The kanban will be the same color as the store location color (i.e., if the store location is yellow, then the kanban should also be yellow).

Put the following information on both sides of the parts withdrawal/supply kanban:

| | | |
|---|---|---|
| 1. | Store Address | Storage location of product |
| 2. | Use Address | Use location of product |
| 3. | Part Name | Name of part |
| 4. | Part # | Part number |
| 5. | Color | Color of part if necessary |
| 6. | Color Block | Color block will be same color as use point color (i.e., if use point location color is purple, then the block will also be purple) |

### Production-Instruction Kanban (PIKB) and Unit Count Boards

A production-instruction kanban (PIKB) is used to signal the operation to produce. It tells operators what to produce and in what quantity. The color of the production-instruction kanban matches the color designation for the primary machine that produces the product. Directions for how to use the production-instruction kanban should be on the back side of the kanban. As Figures 4-5a and 4-5b show, SLMS chose a variable lot kanban system. This is how it works:

A. Inspect the standard WIP or finished goods store for product at or below the yellow line. *The yellow line is the trigger point to move the production instruction to the producing process.* It is acceptable to have SWIP less than the yellow trigger point as long as reorder is in progress.

B. When the yellow line is reached, remove the production-instruction kanban from the WIP address and place it in queue at the producing process. In the case of multiple products that run off the same tool (e.g., different colors of the same product), mark the specifics of the triggering product (e.g., the product color) on the PIKB then place the PIKB in queue.

C. Before a tool change starts, remove the production-instruction kanban from the "tool currently running" location on the press and return it to the marked location on the WIP address line.

D. When the first good part is achieved, enter the number of containers needed to reach the red line. In the case of multiple colors please enter all, even if the trigger point has not been hit on the other colors. Note: If you have multiple colors of a part, it makes sense to run all colors of that part when the tool is in the press, limiting the tool changes. *The red line indicates the maximum inventory level.* Place the kanban in the "tool running" location on the press.

## Tracking the Production

### Unit count board

An operator uses a unit count board to track the production of product against the quantity specified on the production-instruction kanban. A unit count board also indicates color changes, tool changes, or quality checks that must be done. Your machine may have a counter on it to record production; however, it will most likely be too small to see easily. Remember, this is a visual system, so any critical information must be easily viewed by anyone.

One way to ensure high visibility is to construct a unit count board with parallel wires or pipe cleaners strung across a felt-covered board horizontally. On the felt-covered board, string 10 beads on each of the rows of pipe cleaners or wires using two different colors of beads, alternating the color for each row. A colored flag should be hung on the board in a spot representing the number of containers that must be filled to complete the required production-instruction kanban quota.

**SLMS Molding, Inc.**

## Instructions

### Production-Instruction Kanban

1. Inspect standard WIP or finished goods store for product at or below yellow line.

2. When yellow line is reached, remove production-instruction kanban from WIP address line and fill in trigger color only (fill in quantity at Step #5).

3. Place kanban at the machine in next available slot.

4. Before tool change starts, remove production-instruction kanban from "tool running" location on press and return to marked location on WIP address line.

5. When first good shot is achieved, enter number of bins to reach red line for each color. Place kanban in "tool running" location on press.

6. Place red flag on bead count board for number of bins to run. (See bead count board.)

   *Note:* When placing red flag, count from right to left, top to bottom.

7. When designated color and bin quantity have been produced (i.e., the red flag is reached), erase quantity and color from production-instruction kanban.

   **Repeat steps 6 and 7 for each color or item on the production-instruction kanban.**

**Figure 4-5a.** Production Kanban Instructions

---

**SLMS Molding, Inc.**
## Production-Instruction Kanban

Machine: _____

Tool: _____

Material: _____

Part Desc.: _____

| Color | # of Container/Pkg. Required |
|-------|------------------------------|
| _____ | _____ |
| _____ | _____ |
| _____ | _____ |

**Figure 4-5b.** Production-Instruction Kanban

Each bead represents a container. A designated worker counts from top to bottom and from the right side of the board to the left and slides a bead to the right each time a container is filled, repeating the process until the flag is reached. When the flag is reached, the worker stops and notifies the team leader or supervisor it is time to change to the next production-instruction kanban.

In Figure 4-6, the flag is placed after the 28th bead, indicating that the production-instruction kanban calls for 28 containers of the product. Figure 4-7 shows the board after seven containers have been filled. The unit count board shows clearly what to produce, what has been produced, and when to stop producing. It indicates to the operator when a change is coming up, and it provides simple, clear communication between shifts and to anyone walking by what the status of production is at the station or cell.

## Buffer and Safety Stock Kanbans

Buffer and safety stocks are described in Chapter 1. You create these stocks to ensure that you can meet customer demand if it fluctuates significantly from normal buying patterns or when your own system fails temporarily. There are special kanbans you use when you withdraw and replace buffer and safety stock. As noted in the Buffer and Safety Stock section of Chapter 1, these kanbans must be clearly different from the kanbans used for normal production. You must also be able to distinguish between the buffer and safety kanbans. See Figures 4-8 and 4-9 for examples.

## An Additional Visual Communication Structure

This book has already discussed the visual layout and address system, the operator instruction sheets, and the color-coded kanban system, all of which are visual approaches to ensure standardization of the production processes. But you need to keep in mind that the entire pull production system is a visual communication system. For this reason, you may need to create some important visual structures that support operators as they function within the pull system and allow them to communicate the status of production as well as signal when something goes wrong. One of these structures is a *Production Tally Board*. This board will give an overview of the status of production and keep operators informed on how they are performing to target based on takt time. Two other critical communication structures—the heijunka box and the raw material order board—will be discussed in the next chapter, which addresses how to simplify production control and initiate the pull system in your value streams.

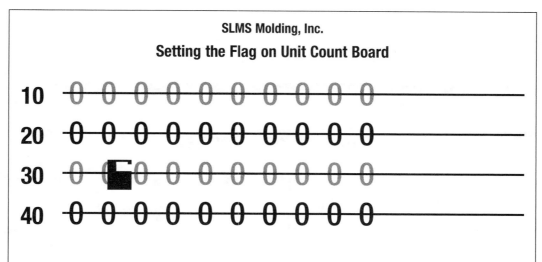

**Figure 4-6.** Unit Count Board

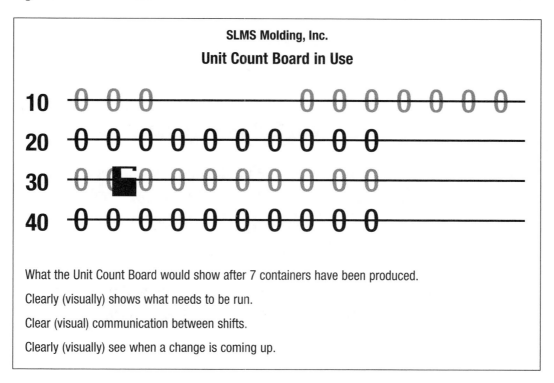

**Figure 4-7.** Unit Count Board in Use

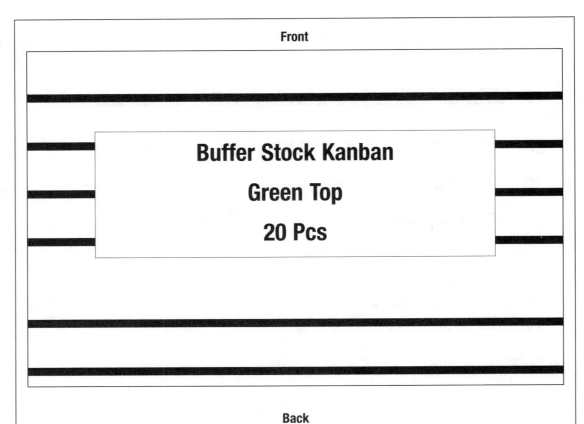

**Front**

# Buffer Stock Kanban

# Green Top

# 20 Pcs

**Back**

## Removal from Buffer Inventory

Please give this Buffer Kanban to the Production Control Department when you remove this container from Buffer Inventory.

## Removal from Heijunka Box

Please place this Buffer Kanban into the container and place the container in the Buffer Inventory in Date Rotation Order.

**Figure 4-8.** Buffer Stock Kanban

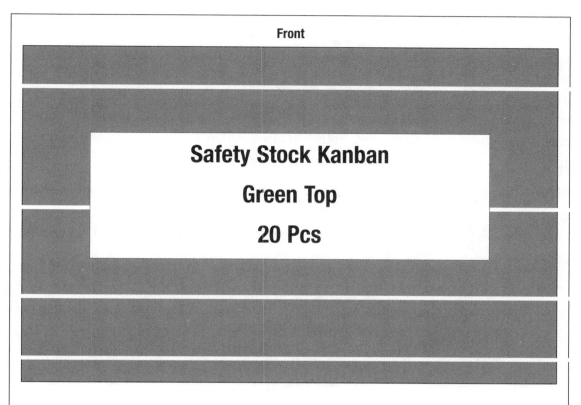

**Front**

# Safety Stock Kanban

## Green Top

## 20 Pcs

**Back**

# Removal from Safety Stock Inventory

When you remove this container from the Safety Inventory:

- Notify the appropriate authority
- Fill out the Safety Stock Log
- Please give this Safety Stock kanban to the department manager

# Removal from Heijunka Box

Please place this Safety Stock kanban into the container and place the container in the Safety Stock Inventory in Date Rotation Order.

**Figure 4-9.** Safety Stock Kanban

### Production tally boards

A production tally board is an inexpensive visual aid that allows teams to understand how they are doing against a production target. It may be a dry-erase board, located at the job site, on which hourly targets are set in relation to takt time. The supervisor, team leader, or another designated worker records the production against the target each hour, along with a brief description of any problem or abnormal condition that arose if the production target was not met.

SLMS used a production tally board as a visual communication tool for operators to gauge their progress and as an information base for the team leader. An example of the company's production tally board is shown in Figure 4-10; Figure 4-11 shows the board in use.

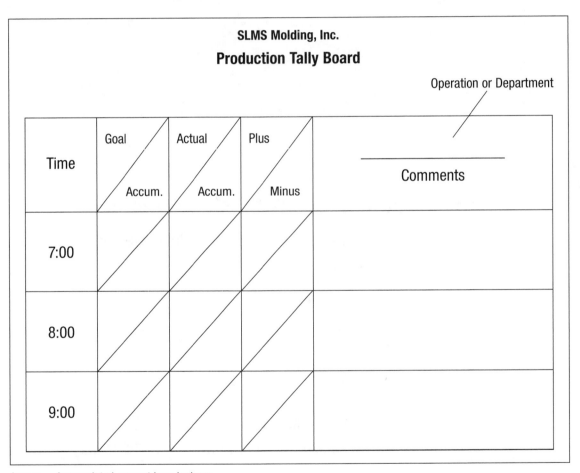

Accum. = Accumulated amount hour by hour

**Figure 4-10.** Production Tally Board

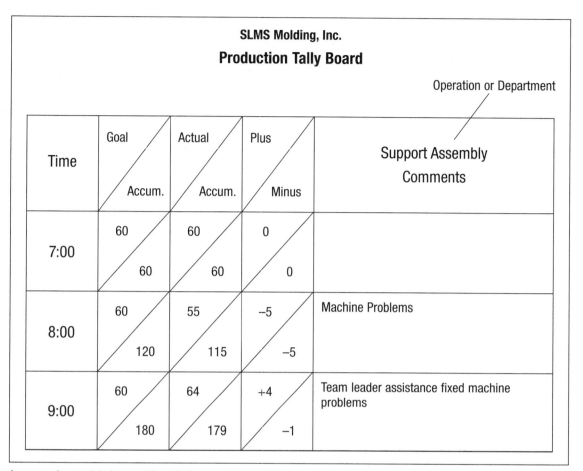

Accum. = Accumulated amount hour by hour

**Figure 4-11.** Production Tally Board in Use

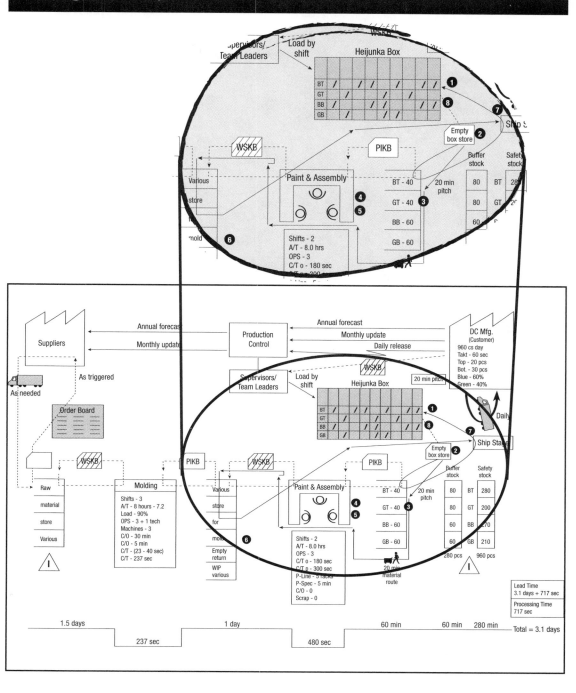

# Chapter 5. Load Leveling, or Heijunka, and the Material Handler

Leveling is the heart and soul of a lean manufacturing system. The key reason for establishing a level pace of production is to enable you to make what is needed when it is needed in the quantity needed. When this is accomplished, you will have a standardized process that, by its very nature, will advise you of problems within the flow and allow you to take immediate corrective action. Moreover, leveling creates the base from which all effective kaizen can be implemented. Thus, load leveling, or heijunka, has incredible potential to respond to many of the variations of production planning and scheduling. The SLMS heijunka is a fairly simple example of this system.

Heijunka (in Japanese, this term means load leveling and balancing) is the best-kept secret of all the Toyota Production System's tools and is the most difficult to understand. Heijunka is the beginning as well as the end of your pull production system. Heijunka sets the pace of flow in production and product withdrawal. The pace of production and withdrawal is equal to the pace of sales. Toyota developed this method of scheduling a plant's activity to smooth out the uneven demand of vehicle variety and volume in order to create mixed-model production.

Heijunka will not work unless you have the first two Ss (Stabilize and Standardize) in place. This means that you will not be able to use a heijunka system until you have completed most of the other steps in the process described in the previous chapters of this workbook. Refer to the heijunka checklist in Figure 5-1 to make sure you have the prerequisites in place for setting up the heijunka box for your value stream.

## How the Heijunka Box Works

Using the heijunka box, you withdraw product from the end of the production line according to an established increment of time—takt time or pitch. You should already have determined the takt time and pitch for the value stream you are transforming.

Production control determines the number of withdrawal kanbans to place in the heijunka box for each shift. The heijunka box is loaded with the orders for each shift

---

**Heijunka Checklist**

1. Has takt time been established based on customer withdrawal?

2. Has pitch been established for the pick-up route schedule based on container quantities?

3. Is there an address system established for the facility and material stores?

4. Are the workstations color coded?

5. Is there a material handler timed to a standard route based on pitch?

6. Is the material handler cart set up properly? Kanbans created?

7. Is the color-coded kanban system in place and everyone trained in its use?

8. Behind schedule signal? Wait Box in place?

9. Buffer and Safety Stock in place?

10. Is standard work established?

---

**Figure 5-1.** Heijunka Checklist

daily, at the beginning of each shift. The box can be loaded by a production control person, team leader, supervisor or a designated person intimate with that value stream. The box contains customer orders identified by actual customer kanbans or labels or a representative of the customer order. These orders are removed by the material handler, in the case of SLMS every 20 minutes, to initiate parts withdrawal and production cycles in accordance with customer demand.

## Heijunka Box Construction

Simple materials can be used to construct the heijunka box. You can use anything that gives you the ability to set up a box that will allow you to see increments of time (pitch) easily. SLMS, for example, used common VHS videotape boxes and built a master container to hold the required quantity of the VHS boxes.

The heijunka box should be set up with one row for each product variation or for each customer of each product. The row labels should include the name of the product or customer, the number of pieces per container, and the color of the product (or other product variant) if applicable. It will have one column for each pitch increment. To calculate the correct number of time slots, or columns, multiply the number of pitch intervals per hour times the number of hours in the shift (see Figure 5-2 for an example of SLMS's calculation).

| Heijunka Calculation at SLMS |
| --- |
| SLMS operates two shifts of 8 hours each |
| We have a pitch of 20 minutes |
| 3 pitches per hour × 8 hours = 24 pitches or slots required + 2 for OT or delay. |
| We have 4 items or part numbers; therefore, 4 rows of boxes will be required. |

**Figure 5-2.** Heijunka Time-Slot Calculation at SLMS

In the case of SLMS, the pitch was 20 minutes, so the time indicator on the heijunka box is 20 minutes (see Figure 5-3). If there is more than one pitch increment in use (e.g., a 10-minute pitch and a 20-minute pitch), you would set up the box using the lower of the pitch increments (in this case, 10-minute intervals).

Standard Lean Manufacturing Systems, Inc.
**Heijunka Box**

| Time / Part | 7:00 | 7:20 | 7:40 | 8:00 | 8:20 | 8:40 | 9:00 | 9:20 | 9:40 | 10:00 | 10:20 | 10:40 | 11:00 | |
| --- | --- | --- | --- | --- | --- | --- | --- | --- | --- | --- | --- | --- | --- | --- |
| Blue Top 20 pcs | | | | | | | | | | | | | | |
| Green Top 20 pcs | | | | | | | | | | | | | | |
| Blue Bottom 30 pcs | | | | | | | | | | | | | | |
| Green Bottom 30 pcs | | | | | | | | | | | | | | |

**Figure 5-3.** Heijunka Box Construction

Normally there should be no more than one kanban per slot in the heijunka box. You will want to create one heijunka for each value stream. One company the authors worked with has 15 lines and 15 heijunkas—one for each line.

## Loading the Heijunka Box—Calculating the Production Sequence

The production sequence should represent the pace of customer withdrawal, and you will need to recalculate it whenever customer requirements change. To facilitate loading the heijunka box, create a production sequence table (see Figure 5-4) and post it at the heijunka box to show the sequence of kanbans needed. For each product, calculate the time it takes to produce enough finished goods to fill one container. Use the following formula:

Minutes to fill one container = (pieces/container) × Takt time / 60 seconds

The example below illustrates how this formula is applied:

Blue Top:    20 pieces/box × 60 seconds / 60 seconds = 20 minutes to fill each container
That is, the customer needs a box of Blue Tops every 20 minutes.

Blue Bottom:    30 pieces/box × 60 seconds / 60 seconds = 30 minutes to fill each container
That is, the customer needs a box of Blue Bottoms every 15 minutes.

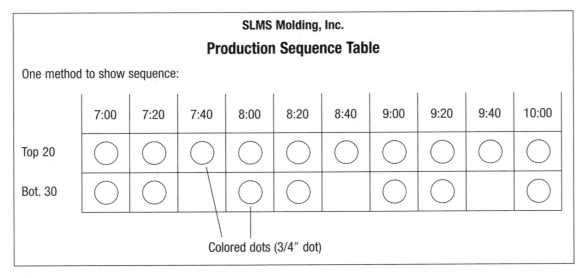

**Figure 5-4.** Production Sequence Table

If pitch is 20 minutes (remember, it should be the lower of the two), then the production sequence will correspond to the table in Figure 5-4.

## Setting the Pace Based on Pitch and Loading the Heijunka Box

Pitch, based on takt time, sets the pace of withdrawal. In order for you to supply your customer appropriately, you must go to the lowest pitch possible. As shown in Figure 5-5, SLMS chose a 20-minute pitch. If the company had set the pitch at 30 minutes to accommodate the bottoms, it would have missed the withdrawal of tops set at 20 minutes.

---

### Pitch for DC  Mfg., Inc.

DC has two pack quantities: 20 and 30

20 pack quantity $\times$ takt time of 60 seconds = 20-minute pitch

30 pack quantity $\times$ takt time of 60 seconds = 30-minute pitch

---

**Figure 5-5.** Pitch at SLMS for DC Manufacturing, Inc.

Figure 5-6 shows how the heijunka box was loaded at SLMS. Note that in the first pitch increment, there is a request for one box of blue tops (20) and one box of blue bottoms (30). In order to keep the customer supplied when the pitch is uneven due to different pack quantities, you normally would pull the larger quantity a bit earlier.

SLMS Molding
**Heijunka Box**

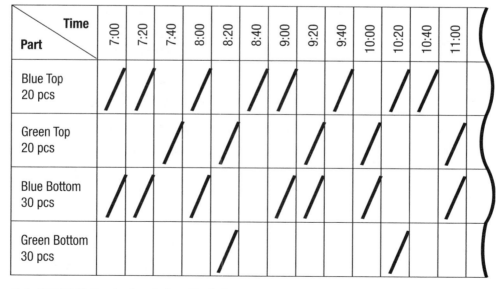

**Figure 5-6.** SLMS Heijunka Loaded to Pitch Sequence

Because there is no 30-minute spot on the heijunka, waiting for equal time would mean missing the delivery.

### Behind Schedule Condition

Management must ensure that the manufacturing system maintains the one-to-one manufacturing process—that is the *move one, make one* pull production strategy in which production is triggered by a customer order. In the event that the system falls behind schedule, all efforts must be made to stabilize the process and make up for any lost production. This is accomplished by assigning additional help to the production line. This assistance must be supplied by management and cannot interfere with the normal material-handling pattern. All additional WIP needed to catch up and all finished product must be replaced or withdrawn by the assisting team members.

The signal for a behind schedule condition is an *andon* light, flag, and/or sound located at each operation. When a box of finished goods or product is not available for withdrawal, the *andon* is activated by the material handler, signaling to management that something is wrong—a behind schedule condition exists. Management must react in a timely manner to ensure the problem is fixed immediately.

### Wait Box

A wait box is used to maintain the production order while the behind schedule condition is being remedied by the assisting team members. If product is not available, the protocol is to place the withdrawal kanban in pocket #1 of the wait box (see Figure 5-7) and activate the andon—raise the flag, sound the horn or play the music, and/or turn on the light—to notify the production manager that a problem has arisen.

If product continues to be unavailable, kanbans are placed in the wait box pockets in sequence—#2, #3, etc. As product becomes available, team members can remove the wait kanbans, starting with the lowest number (the earliest one placed in the wait box) and resume production until the wait box is empty and the process is back on schedule. If you fail to make up the lost production, you must pull the material from safety stock inventory to complete the customer order on time.

The material handler ensures that pitch is maintained. You must treat the cycle time that the material handler needs to complete a route the same as you would any other timed element. The material handler must have time to complete all elements of a given job within the pitch time established. You develop the route structure after confirming the time. This may take several iterations to determine the most effective and efficient route. The material handler starts by removing kanbans (customer orders)

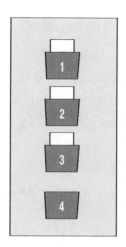

SLMS Molding
**Withdrawal Kanban Wait Box**

If the product is not ready, please place the withdrawal kanban in pocket #1.

**Raise the signal flag** (if a flag is used).

If product continues to be unavailable, continue to place the kanbans in the pockets, 2, 3, etc.

As product becomes available, please remove the wait kanbans starting with the lowest number and place the current kanban in the next available pocket in the withdrawal kanban wait box.

Please continue to do this until the shortage is rectified.

**Figure 5-7.** Wait Box

from the heijunka box. These are visual work orders that tell the material handler how much and what products to move to the ship stage for customer pickup. In most cases, the material handler uses the supply/withdrawal production kanbans to pick up and deliver appropriate raw materials to the production line.

Moving in a circular route through the value stream from ship stage through final assembly and production cells to the raw material stage and back again, the material handler resembles a water spider spinning on the surface of a mountain stream. As the flow of production moves smoothly downstream, pulled by the force of customer demand, the water spider spins from racks to cells to racks to cells, creating a circular pattern on the surface of the value stream and keeping the flow of production smooth and level.

A review of the material handler's route at SLMS gives a detailed example of how it works. As you saw in Chapter 2, SLMS figured out how many parts should be in each container of material and how many containers should be on the line-side racks at the paint/assembly cell. In the section on pitch in Chapter 1, you learned that the material handler serving this value stream must walk a replenishment route or loop of 20 minutes to match the pitch. Putting the pull system in motion begins with the material handler and the loaded heijunka box.

## Heijunka Box: Steps 1 and 2 of Future State Map

The material handler's route starts at the heijunka box. It is here that the handler picks up withdrawal kanbans indicating what finished goods (i.e., customer orders) to pick from the paint and assembly cell. The handler then moves to the empty box store to get empty boxes that match the customer orders.

## Finished Goods Supermarket: Step 3 of Future State Map

At the paint and assembly cell, the material handler picks containers (i.e., finished goods) corresponding to the withdrawal kanbans and places the containers on the cart. The handler places the production-instruction kanban into the empty box and puts it on the assembly line. He or she then puts the customer kanban in the full box and moves the box to the cart.

## Material Racks at Cells: Steps 4 and 5 of Future State Map

The handler then moves to the material racks at the paint and assembly cell and picks up the kanbans and empty containers from the assembly racks, indicating what raw material must be replaced. He or she places the color-coded kanbans into the color-coded sleeves on the cart. The colors correspond to storage areas in the raw materials supermarket.

## Raw Material Racks: Step 6 of Future State Map

The material handler then walks the cart to the raw material supermarket between molding and assembly, retrieves the required raw material containers, and places the supply withdrawal kanbans into the raw material containers (see Figure 5-8). He then wheels the cart back to the appropriate racks in assembly as indicated by the line-side address and color code on the kanbans. The handler drops off any empty raw material containers in the empty container lane at the molding supermarket.

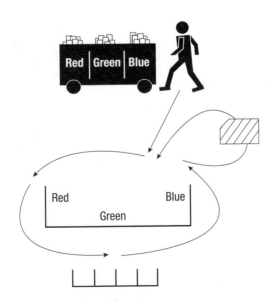

**Figure 5-8.** Material Handler at Raw Material Supermarket.

## Ship Stage: Steps 7 and 8 of Future State Map

Finally the material handler places the finished goods from the cart, picked up at the start of the route, into the ship stage area and returns to the heijunka box to pick up kanbans for the next route.

## Activity at the Assembly Cell

In the assembly cell, as an operator starts to assemble a support arm, he or she needs a new box of parts. The operator sends the empty box down a slide, pulls a withdrawal kanban from a new container of needed parts, and places it on a kanban post for the material handler to pick up. The handler picks up the withdrawal kanban and goes "shopping" in the raw material supermarket between assembly and the molding presses. The color-coded kanban has a pick-up address and color for the supermarket and a line-side color and delivery address. The handler picks up a new container of parts from the supermarket, carefully replacing the withdrawal kanban in the plastic envelope on the front of the container. The handler brings the new box of parts to the assembly cell and puts it in the rack. By that time, the operator has used the parts in the box, so he or she removes the empty container from the storage rack and places it on a separate rack for the material handler to pick up. There is now an empty space for the new container that the handler is bringing back.

This paced process creates a flow of production activity that is smooth and without waste. It will take some time to get it working this precisely, but when you do, the hum of the value stream and the beat of customer orders will sound like a symphony.

# Stage III. Simplify

To simplify your processes, you must have first completed the work described in the Stabilize and Standardize sections because this establishes the foundation from which effective kaizen can begin. Companies that do not establish this foundation seldom achieve their goals as well as expected. Although they create kaizen events, these are all too often directed at "cosmetic implementation" rather than simplification.

Cosmetic or unsustainable implementation is akin to a tree with shallow roots. The first slight wind and the tree falls. Unless everyone in the organization has grasped lean concepts and philosophy, your efforts will fail. Simplification or kaizen will be a continuing process in your lean effort. Companies that do not cultivate this understanding frequently fall prey to the "quick fix" syndrome, which is the greatest enemy of lean. Many companies, for example, initiate improvement with an approach called kaizen blitz. This is a short-term, crash-and-burn approach to simplification that may have some impact on the area involved. In most cases, the implemented change is not sustainable over a long period of time. This process takes people (both those in management and on the shop floor) out of their comfort zone and there is a tendency to backtrack as soon as something goes even slightly awry. When this occurs, people return to the comforting familiarity of the "old ways" instead of facing and fixing problems.

One example of the quick fix syndrome shows how ineffective it can be. Consider what is likely to happen when a department supervisor or team leader announces, "Senior management is coming to see our progress on the lean workshop that we just completed. We need to get some visual address cards in place." The team puts the visual cards in place and does not review the program with the shop floor. Training is not complete, but things look good when senior management shows up. In short order, the cosmetic system falls apart because the team did not have a plan to make sure the training process was completed.

Cosmetic implementation via quick fixes poses another problem. It sends a signal that management does not take the lean initiative seriously. The quickest way to have your operators conclude that this is just another "flavor of the month program" is through unsustainable quick fixes. Deterioration is inevitable, and eventually, everyone reverts to the old way.

Creating conditions that allow you to see the operational environment is a key part of the lean effort, and this means paying scrupulous attention to visual indicators that make it easy to understand where you are and what you have to do. Meaningful and consistent address systems, operator instruction sheets, production-instruction kanbans, unit count boards, labor balance charts, etc., all give you the ability to see what is going on in your plant.

Standing and watching processes, not just for a few minutes, but for an extended period of time, will also allow you to understand the issues you need to understand and take corrective action accordingly. Enlisting the assistance of the operators in this process is essential. They know the problems and their input on what needs to be changed and simplified will be invaluable. This is a collaborative effort, and all departments must participate! Above all, everyone must understand that your first future state is not the end of the lean journey. It is a new current state that will forever require transformation into a new future state.

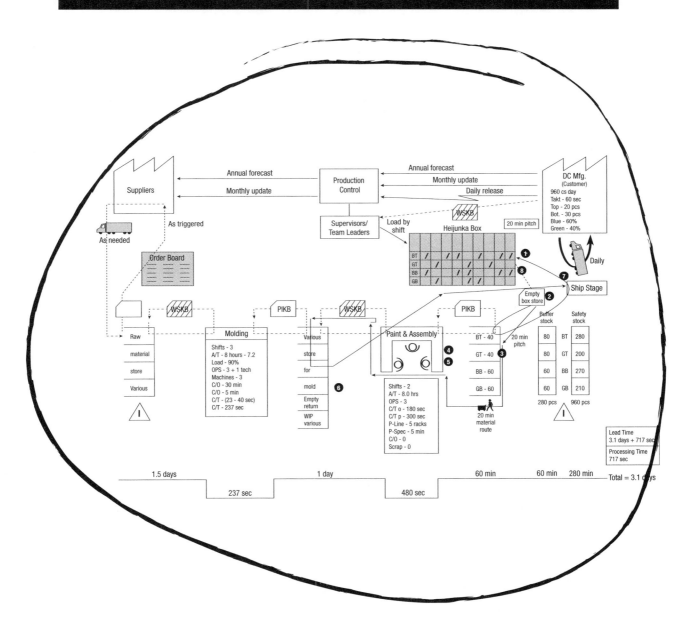

# Chapter 6. Opportunities for Simplification

Establishing paced withdrawal lets you see which areas need attention (after you have resolved the obvious issues). This paced withdrawal is based on your pitch and the use of a heijunka box, as explained in Chapter 5. When you have introduced heijunka into your operation, you have created the conditions that will enable you to see the weak links in your flow and start the simplification process.

## An Approach to Simplification

"Simplify" has multiple meanings, all of which can be related to lean activities. Stroll through an operation or cell. Observe and continuously challenge the current state by asking yourself what can be done

- to make things simpler;
- to make things easier;
- to shorten;
- to reduce to the bare bones.

These basic definitions have been around for a long time, but if you truly want to take advantage of the opportunities they suggest, you must begin by looking at what exists. This same rule applies to middle managers and line managers in your plant. Senior executives should (must) spend at least one hour on the shop floor every day across shifts. When was the last time you took a lean walk through your plant on an off shift? Middle managers should (must) spend four hours on the shop floor every day across shifts. Line managers must spend eight hours on the shop floor. Paperwork documenting what was observed must by completed.

For many of you reading this, the immediate response to this will be, "We don't have that kind of time!" The answer to this is that the time exists and should be found and used. Consider, for example, the line balance activities when you determine the staffing for the assembly line. It is divided into value and non-value added time. Much the same can be said of any activity in any location or function of your company. Find the time that is available and use it wisely. You will, in the process, discover that the time you spend reducing waste will give you even more time to devote to improvement and to implementation of the most powerful change that you can make in your plant to increase profitability.

Review the seven major wastes—motion, inventory, defects, transportation, overproduction, waiting, extra processing. Burn them into your brain. Then start looking for them and at them and ask what can be done to simplify and reduce their impact.

## Examples of Simplification

Simplifying does not have to involve a major kaizen event. It means observing the on-site activities of people or processes and continuously asking, "Why?"

- Why am I not on the shop floor?
- Why are we missing pitch?
- Why are we doing this?
- Why am I doing it this way?
- Why are we handling it this way?
- Why is that operator having to _____?
- Why is the operator leaving the line?
- Why does it take so long for the material handler to complete his route?

In the answers to these questions, you will find many opportunities for simplification. Each of the following examples is typical of a problem that many manufacturers encounter. Each can be resolved by asking the right "why?"

### Issue: Difficulty in Presenting Parts to the Assembly Line Operator

A team could not place material needed by the operator in a convenient place because air cylinders for the fixtures were in the way. Why? Available space was not being utilized in the best way. After reviewing the table that held the fixtures, the team realized that there was nothing *under* the table. They moved the air cylinders under the table so there was no interference with placing the needed materials within easy reach of the operator.

### Issue: Waste of Movement (Excessive Walking)

When the existing large containers were placed on the line, they caused additional walking for the operator. Why? The containers took up too much space. The team reviewed lot sizes, meaning the quantity placed in each container. They reduced the lot size so smaller containers could be used. (In instances where you are not able to change the packaging from the supplier, you may have the material handler remove the materials from the container to the appropriate box for the line until you can change the packaging.)

### Issue: Waste of Movement (Excessive Walking)

Operators on an assembly line producing a large product had to make multiple trips to the plant supermarket to obtain parts. Why? The parts were not always needed at the same time. A mini-market was set up on the side of the line, and the assemblers were given a shopping basket with specific places in which they would put the materials that they needed to build the part, reducing the walking time by 80 percent.

### Issue: Waste of Movement (Excessive Walking)

Operators on a seat assembly line were walking a great distance to get small parts to complete their tasks. Why? There were quite a few parts and a variety of colors for the same part, each kept in a separate location. The team reviewed the process and decided that a material handler could place the exact parts required into a kit, then place the kit on the conveyor, thus eliminating the need for the assembler to search for the needed part.

### Issue: Overproduction

Operators at one station (A) were overproducing subassemblies for the next station (B). They were then placing the excess subassemblies on the floor, which resulted in defects. Why? When this situation occurs, it is usually an indication that there may be excess labor at station B and the situation needs a review. New time studies revealed that the operators at station A could perform the tasks at a cycle time that was faster than takt time. The line was rebalanced, removing one operator.

### Issue: Excess Inventory

A riveting machine produced a complex mix of products for its in-plant customer. Significant inventory built up between the two operations. Why? There was considerable distance between the two operations. A team conducted a major study to determine whether they could move the machine in line with the next operation, eliminating the need for inventory. A study of cycle times, changeover times, and operator movement determined that the move could be made. The team put in place a replenishment system that sent multiple signals in a sequenced order to the producing process without the use of a computer. This was designed to sequence the demand from the customer to the riveting machine. This system enabled the operator to produce exactly what the customer removed on a one-for-one basis. WIP inventories were eliminated and space was freed up; this space was used for additional equipment for a new product.

### Issue: The Material Handler Was Not Able to Complete the Loop in Pitch Time

The material handler had a problem in easily identifying addresses for parts pickup. Why? All the supply/withdrawal kanbans were the same color. The team adopted a color-coding system for kanbans, which enabled the material handler to complete the loop within pitch time.

### Issue: Excess Transport, Random Delivery Forklift Traffic

This can occur in a large plant with multiple forklift trucks and material handlers delivering raw materials and removing finished goods. Why? Random routes. Consider a bus route system or a commuter train in which specific routes are established on a time basis to pick up and drop off passengers. The same type of system can be developed to deliver product and take away finished goods from your line. This will give you direct control over the movement of traffic in the plant.

### Issue: Extra Processing (Waste) Because of Customer Package Requirements

The customer requires that 60 parts be packed in a container, but your lot size is only five. When a lot size of five parts is completed, the operator marks a part with a ticket or marker to ensure that the count is correct. This is an extra step, which is waste. Why? Focus on the parts and not the container. The team put a unit count board in place. When the lot of five parts was completed, the operator moved a bead on the board. The time required to move the bead was substantially less than using the marker or ticket. When 12 beads had been moved, the container was complete and the beads were moved back to the start position on the board.

### Issue: Insufficient Capacity

A line manager requested a lean team to review a three-shift assembly line that was running at capacity. Why? Cycle time was too long. The team came up with a new way to structure the assembly line, reducing cycle time. However, the plan required a new, untested piece of equipment. Because of the need to meet customer demand, the team could not interrupt operations to test the new idea on the line, so team members created a mock-up of the new assembly line structure using cardboard and foam blocks. They called in the workers from one shift two hours early and asked them to simulate their activities based on the new line concept. Using this method, the team was able to test their ideas, get operator participation, and determine whether the ideas made sense—all without interrupting normal production.

## Ongoing Simplification

Some simplification efforts do not require major kaizen events. For example, you can check whether wheels on delivery carts are too small for ease of movement or whether visual controls are in place so abnormal activity can be easily detected and corrected.

You will see more opportunities as you continuously improve your operation. Obstacles will pop up that must be overcome. When you set up your new operational environment, all things will not work perfectly; mistakes will be made. Remember that this is part of the learning process. It will be a test of your resolve to remain committed to your never-ending journey of lean implementation. You will get frustrated because you will miss pitches; initially, you may have only an 80 percent success rate. Stay the course: Continue to simplify, and your organization will continue to improve the quality of life in your plant and dramatically improve profits. Lean implementation is not a "project"—it is a lifelong quest for excellence and waste elimination.

# Chapter 7. Q & A

Some of the more common problems you may encounter are covered in the Frequently Asked Questions presented below. Please note that the answers provided are not the only answers. The authors have taken their cue here from Toyota whose response to such questions is almost invariably, "That is one answer." The response is a good one because it clearly indicates that every problem can have more than one solution. For this reason, it is important to keep an open mind to ideas for change or improvement to a process. Listen to your team members. Their suggestions may lead to a better method. Build on each other's strengths so that you can continuously improve the process.

**My customer wants me to maintain a large finished-goods inventory.**

Initially, put in place a finished-goods inventory that will satisfy the customer. As you gain in confidence and ability to meet demand—and as you prove that you have that ability—you can start a planned reduction of this inventory.

**What do I do if the customer orders more product than I can make in a shift or day?**

Pull the excess demand from the buffer stock. Use the next available sequence to replenish your buffer.

**My system failed, and I had to pull from safety stock. How do I replenish?**

When you pull material from safety stock, you will normally have to work overtime to replenish your inventory.

**How do I replenish my buffer stock?**

Under normal circumstances your buffer inventory will be replenished automatically. When the customer pulls more, you use the buffer; when the customer pulls less, you refill the buffer.

### How do I handle chronic failure in my value stream?

You can place a small buffer of material downstream from the process that is out of control to support flow. However, you must have an agreed-upon removal date so the buffer does not become a crutch or the problem will never get resolved.

### I do not have enough space for my WIP.

Make certain you have calculated the lot size correctly. You may, in some circumstances, have to store the WIP in another area.

### OK, but where?

As near as possible to the material handler's route.

### One operator is slower (or faster) than another on the same job. How do I handle that?

You should use the most frequent/repeatable cycle to establish a baseline. Use reasonable judgment. Work with the operators, videotape the process, discuss the problems and issues. You may want to use your best operator to assist and/or train the slower operator. Please understand some people are not as skillful or adept as others and may not be able to do some tasks. If you have a cell and the operators rotate within that cell, you might consider skipping the slower operator when assigning work to a given position in the rotation.

### My material handler cannot make the route in time.

Study the route to see if you can find obstacles or other wastes. Initially, you may have to place two material handlers on the route.

### Sometimes a part rejected by the supplier gets to the line. What do I do?

A team leader should get a replacement and advise the appropriate person or department of the problem. Do not let the operator get a replacement!

### What do I do if a kanban gets lost?

This may happen, but you can keep the frequency under control by stressing the importance of kanbans and their role in managing the system. Replace the lost kanban with a new kanban that indicates it is a duplicate. This avoids any confusion if the original shows up.

**Should my improvement processes be sequential or parallel?**

You have to review your future state plan and use common sense to determine which areas can parallel each other and which must be sequential. For instance, you should not try to balance an assembly operation until you have determined takt time. SLMS did not establish lot sizes in the containers until determining the pitch of the pull.

**How will lean affect my Six Sigma program?**

Lean is a philosophy, whereas Six Sigma is a tool that supports this philosophy. When you have a foundation based on lean concepts, you will be able to use Six Sigma more effectively.

**How will lean affect my TPM and TQM programs?**

As with Six Sigma, these are tools. The more you understand the lean concept of flow, the better you can apply these tools.

With patience and dedication, the systems will work. You will be establishing a flow that requires capable processes. Initially, you will see system failure, which will cause many to doubt the concept and philosophy. Use reasonable judgment in your decision-making process, but do not be afraid to stretch the envelope.

# Index

# About the Authors

**Tom Luyster** is the president of SLMS, Inc., an organization dedicated to assisting the manufacturing community in implementing lean concepts and systems. Before founding SLMS, Inc., Tom held senior executive positions in manufacturing and sales. During his training in the Toyota Production System (TPS) philosophy under H. Ohba and K. Fukunaga of the Toyota Supplier Support Center (TSSC), Tom was instrumental in establishing the benchmark U.S. facility that TSSC uses in its TPS training workshops. He has been recognized by Toyota for his TPS presentation to the Pacific Rim Supplier Group.

Tom's goal is to help clients implement their version of lean-based manufacturing, using a simple philosophy of stability, standardization, and simplification with TPM and TQM tools. He and his team have implemented successful and profit-increasing lean conversions in a wide spectrum of domestic and international industries including injection molding, metal stamping, tube and tire manufacturing, medical devices, brake systems, die casting, furniture, aerospace and others. He is the co-author of *Value Stream Management* (Productivity Press, 2002).

**Don Tapping** has worked more than twenty-five years to eliminate waste and improve bottom-line results. Don is a co-author of *Value Stream Management for the Lean Office* (Productivity Press, 2003), *Who Hollered Fore?*, and numerous other books on business performance, setting the bar for administrative lean improvements. He continues to enlighten organizations with his ability to design step-by-step implementation methodologies identifying processes that require improvement and then introducing  proactive steps to improve or redesign them — reducing costs, boosting performance, and increasing customer satisfaction. Don has a consulting and publishing company with affiliates in Chelsea, Michigan, and Venice, Florida. He has a B.A. from the University of Michigan and an MBA from the University of Notre Dame.